Four Years in a Cave: Surviving Genocide

By

Julian Bhebhe

Dedication

I dedicate *Four Years in a Cave* to Zee, a champion of courage, a man of valor, a man who escaped torture and successfully hid from a bloodthirsty military. Zee refused to be killed for a fake crime and, with boldness, informs the world about what transpired. I also honor the late Joe, a selfless individual who, together with his wife, despite the little they had, willingly provided sustenance to the brave survivor. Without Joe, Zee would have starved to death in a cave, possibly devoured by wild animals, or apprehended and torn to pieces by the heartless murderers.

Acknowledgement

My gratitude goes to the chief character who strangely opened his heart to share a difficult and painful experience that he vehemently withheld from the most informed, persistent, and persuasive individuals in the community. Hopefully, the horrid survival in a cave exposes those responsible for the brutality against a defenseless minority group. Further indebtedness goes to Joe's and Zee's wives, including Zee's now-deceased uncle, for corroborating and concealing Zee's story until the end of the military madness.

About the Author

Julian Bhebhe is an organization development practitioner and teaches online business communication in higher education. He holds a master's degree in communication from Regent University and an Ed.D. in organizational leadership from the University of Phoenix. Julian is an Organization Development Certified Professional through the Institute of Organization Development.

Contents

Introduction

A former elementary school teacher survives the genocide in the 1980s in Zimbabwe. The ordeal takes place when the new Black government engages in a campaign to eliminate a minority tribe. The small grouping, with its distinct language, supports the opposition party that threatens the majority ruling party.

The main character, the survivor, belongs to the minority tribe. As an influential member of the community, the state considers him an obstacle to the advancement of the ruling agenda. Without warning, soldiers fabricate a charge accusing him of collaborating with the dissidents to undermine the government. Subsequently, soldiers raid his school, arrest him, and torture him, but he manages to escape.

The brutal arrest marks the beginning of a military purge designed to annihilate members of the minority tribe under the pretext of weeding out dissidents. Under the guise of eliminating dissidents, defenseless civilians are accused of hiding the enemy and are murdered ruthlessly. The situation worsens when soldiers engage informers in communities to report anyone suspected of feeding dissidents. In a similar manner, the survivor is falsely accused and abducted to ensure that he dies like anyone hated or envied in the community. To this day, the betrayer and the motive for the betrayal remain mysteries.

While the survivor is arrested, the newly formed military brigade continues to cause havoc to the defenseless minority tribe, leaving tens of thousands dead. Despite the loss of life in the region, the world remains silent.

Following his escape from torture for a crime he did not commit, the survivor hides in a cave for four years. He hides to protect his family. At the same time, he loses control of his property as he languishes on the level of a helpless wild animal, eluding predators.

While in the cave, only the confidants know that he is alive. Only confidants know where he hides. Only one person he trusts brings him food. Only the trusted can make him feel human and update him on what is going on in the land. If not for this trusted friend, the survivor would have remained in the cave longer than he should have. He moves out of the cave with full information about the provisions of amnesty, hoping for re-employment and a normal life again.

To the survivor's surprise, twists and turns await him outside the cave. To begin with, amnesty carries a new meaning. Amnesty means pardoning those who committed atrocities while denying retirement benefits to anyone who escapes from the soldiers.

After retirement, the survivor has no income to cover medical costs arising from injuries related to torture. For that reason, the survivor appeals for help with the release of his retirement benefits. Further, he demands restitution for the loss of property while hiding and compensation for the pain and suffering endured during the torture for a crime he did not commit.

He wants the world to know that there is ample evidence to prove that the state massacred thousands of defenseless people. The survivor pleads with the United Nations (UN) and the International Criminal Court (ICC) to engage communities where the military brigade operated and collect data on what transpired during the genocide. Acknowledgment of the genocide should lead to the prosecution of those responsible for the killing of thousands of innocent lives and bring closure to the dark past.

Chapter 1
Guerilla War Ends

Politics is a dirty game that politicians play rough with. These shrewd individuals use words to achieve personal goals. They focus on what matters to them. They create problems that do not exist and use words to make the problems sound real. They lie. They deceive, agitate, and manipulate followers to turn against each other for political expediency. In some cases, politicians incite violence and negotiate to achieve personal goals. In the process, innocent lives perish. While people are killing each other, the politicians downplay the clashes as patriotism. They dismiss indescribable atrocities as media distortions. They fight hard to block investigations in their attempts to hide evidence. Politicians cause religious wars, world wars, and racial wars, including tribal wars, and Zimbabwean politicians are no exception.

In the late 19th century, the British colonized Zimbabwe, formerly Rhodesia. The White settlers assumed control of the resources and amassed wealth, while the Black population languished in poverty. The Black population consisted of Shona and Ndebele-speaking groups. The Shona population in the north of the country outnumbered the Ndebele people in the southern part of the country. In the late 1950s and early 1960s, enlightened Black nationalists from both the majority and minority tribes grouped and formed political parties to wrestle power from White dominance. The White rulers frustrated Blacks' efforts to establish enduring political parties. The struggle culminated in the formation of the Zimbabwe African People's Union (ZAPU) in 1961.

Joshua Nkomo, of Ndebele origin, became the leader of ZAPU. The rise of Joshua Nkomo irked some Shona-speaking politicians within ZAPU, leading to a split in 1963. The Shona-speaking politicians formed their own party called the Zimbabwe African National Union (ZANU), led by Robert Mugabe, who eventually became the first African leader of independent Zimbabwe in 1980.

The two parties went on to form military wings to start the Guerilla War against the White Rhodesian Army. ZAPU formed the Zimbabwe Revolutionary People's Army (ZPRA) based in Zambia. ZPRA, consisting of both Ndebele-speaking and Shona-speaking fighters, entered the country from the south, west, and northwest. ZPRA fought in Ndebele-speaking Matabeleland and the central region, the Midlands, where people spoke both Shona and Ndebele. In addition, ZPRA had a presence in the northwest of the country where people spoke Shona.

ZANU, on the other hand, formed the Zimbabwe African National Liberation Army (ZANLA), based in Tanzania and Mozambique. ZANLA fighters infiltrated Rhodesia through the eastern and northeastern regions of the country.

The ZANLA forces, predominantly Shona-speaking, operated in Shona-speaking areas in the northern parts of the country. As the war progressed, ZANLA decided to deploy its fighters through the southeastern region into the southern and central parts of the country. The population in the southern and central parts of the country spoke the Ndebele language and supported ZAPU, led by Joshua Nkomo. That meant the Shona-speaking ZANLA forces would operate in the areas where the Ndebele-speaking people lived. The sudden clash of languages caused tension between the ZANLA fighters and the Ndebele population in the southern and central regions of the country.

The armed ZANLA cadres demanded the locals speak Shona, a language they could not speak or understand. Failure to speak Shona implied that the locals were being defiant, and this gave the guerillas a reason to be violent. Complications escalated when the cadres demanded food and where to deliver the food in the Shona language, which the locals did not understand. Through misunderstanding and fear of asking for clarity, the locals would prepare and serve the wrong food, infuriating the fighters. The cadres interpreted the preparation of the wrong food as defiance. To make matters worse, the people would deliver food to selected rendezvous known as "bases" late and find the cadres hungry and angry. The delays in food delivery would prompt the cadres to abuse the locals for disobedience.

Upon feasting and regaining strength from the food delivered, the cadres educated the locals about ZANU ideology. All able-bodied people, young and old, male and female, were to report to bases for indoctrination when ordered. Indoctrination came through singing revolutionary songs, dancing, and slogan chanting. Recall that the local population in the southern region and parts of the Midlands region supported ZAPU under Joshua Nkomo. Knowing that the locals supported Nkomo, the cadres forced the locals to denounce Joshua Nkomo and magnify Robert Mugabe as a better leader. Further, the cadres beat to death anyone refusing to embrace and exalt Robert Mugabe. It was also at the nighttime gatherings that the fighters raped girls and young women.

The ZANU political education sought to instill fear in the locals to undermine ZAPU support and reinforce ZANU ideology in the southern region and parts of the Midlands. During indoctrination, the guerillas beat up people to disclose the names of those who avoided interaction with the guerillas. To that end, people reported whomever they hated in the villages, and the persons named died for supporting Joshua Nkomo and for allegedly collaborating with the White Rhodesian Army. Anyone accused of conniving with the White administration, even without evidence, earned the label "sellout, spy, or puppet." Punishment for a sellout, a traitor, was through a bullet, torture, and other excruciating means.

Young men became the eyes and ears of the fighters. The young men provided information about the movement and whereabouts of Rhodesian soldiers and ZPRA fighters. The young men were not only vital sources of information to the ZANLA guerillas but to the Rhodesian soldiers and ZPRA forces as well. The intelligence from the young men helped the various fighters hide from each other rather than clash. Knowing that they were essential sources of information, the young men learned to give information that would make the ZANLA guerillas leave their villages. If the guerillas failed to listen to the young men's intelligence, the Rhodesian soldiers would call on the air force to bombard the ZANLA guerillas. If the Rhodesian Air Force killed the ZANLA cadres, under the cover of darkness, the ZANLA guerillas would return to harass the locals for calling the Rhodesian forces to attack the fighters. The truth is that the local population had no influence or control over the Rhodesian Army, ZPRA, or ZANLA operations. The soldiers and fighters did as they saw fit.

What intrigued most young men who relayed information to the fighters was that the Rhodesian soldiers avoided clashes with the ZPRA forces. This practice carried on until the ceasefire, when all forces engaged in the Guerilla War for Independence-ZPRA and ZANLA forces assembled at different points for integration with the Rhodesian military into a single national army.

Integration Challenges

The transfer of power from the White minority regime to the Black majority regime looked morally sound. It looked like the right thing to do. The new leader from the Shona majority tribe chose to reconcile with the former White rulers to lead the country in a new direction. Equally important was the integration of former fighters into a united force.

Uniting the former White Rhodesian Army with the predominantly Shona-speaking ZANLA cadres and the mixed ZPRA forces was a mammoth task. Lack of trust among the former fighters led to misunderstandings during the integration process. Many reports show that the ZANLA commanders frustrated the Ndebele-speaking former ZPRA forces. Consequently, some disgruntled former ZPRA guerillas disserted with weapons.

To contain the situation, the state sent out groups of armed men, to pose as former ZPRA fighters who fled with weapons. The armed men, also labeled *dissidents,* roamed villages in Matabeleland and the Midlands, resorting to banditry. The media portrayed the dissidents as misguided elements seeking to overthrow the government. What confused Ndebele-speaking people in Matabeleland and parts of the Midlands regions was that the dissidents replicated the terror perpetrated by ZANLA fighters during the Guerilla War in Matabeleland and parts of the central regions. People in the regions mentioned wondered why the disgruntled former ZPRA fighters would torment fellow Ndebele speakers. The situation quickly deteriorated to the point where the new and fragile government deployed a specially trained army brigade to hunt down the dissidents in Matabeleland and the Midlands.

The hope for a better life under Black rule was short-lived. Within two years of self-rule, independence lost its meaning. The new government turned against its own Black people. One morning, the people in the southern region of the country woke up to a curfew with helicopters flying above, giving instructions that the residents remain indoors. Foot soldiers went from house to house searching for guns and seizing "*induku*," knobkerries that Ndebele men used as weapons.

After the seizure of weapons from the Ndebele population, the government deployed the Fifth Brigade, also known as the *Gukurahundi,* over the Matabeleland and parts of the Midlands regions, unleashing violence comparable to, if not worse than, the Second World War Holocaust.

In the Shona language, Gukurahundi means "the wind that sweeps away the dust," similar to "rain that washes away the chaff." Thus, the Gukurahundi brigade would cleanse the country of impurity. Gukurahundi would use military force to sweep away anything and anyone threatening the new government. What an opportunity for the newly elected Prime Minister Robert Mugabe to consolidate his power and settle scores with the Ndebele-speaking minority that resented him! Then savagery and anguish ensued.

Chapter 2
Fifth Brigade Unleashed

The new, fragile government wrestled with the integration of former fighters to the point where some fighters absconded with arms. The ZPRA ex-fighters who chose to discontinue integration were frustrated within the army, and only they could explain why they left the army the way they did. The ex-fighters returned to the people, where they received sustenance during the Guerilla War. The people did not understand why the armed deserters were returning to their communities when they should have been integrating into the new army. Nevertheless, the villagers provided the food to avoid harassment by the armed men. When the Fifth Brigade, pursuing the deserters, came to the villages, they got confirmation that dissidents had passed by and demanded food at gunpoint. The villagers did not know who the armed men were, what they were trying to accomplish, or where they were going. The villagers did not condone what the deserters were doing. Moreover, the villagers were tired of war and wanted the government to start rebuilding the country.

The Ndebele people wondered if the armed men were disgruntled former ZPRA fighters, state agents disguising themselves as ex-ZPRA fighters, or outright criminals. The problem was that when the villagers refused to cook for the deserters or the dissidents, the dissidents killed them. If the villagers cooked for the dissidents, the security forces accused them of collaborating with the enemy.

From the state's point of view, the population in Matabeleland and parts of the Midlands was supporting deserters to undermine the new administration. Such action was unacceptable and could only be ended with a firm hand. Then, the state deployed the Fifth Brigade to pursue and apprehend the dissidents.

North Korea agreed to train the Fifth Brigade, a new regiment of the national army. In essence, the predominantly Shona-speaking Gukurahundi brigade was set to eliminate and clean up the armed banditry in Matabeleland and parts of the Midlands regions. At the same time, the special brigade would punish the villagers who collaborated, harbored, and fed the dissidents. Recall that the defenseless villagers harassed at gunpoint and coerced to feed the dissidents were Ndebele-speaking. Accordingly, the new brigade would use ruthless means to extract information from the local population about the dissidents under the pretext of restoring order.

Upon completion of training, the Fifth Brigade deployed its units to different parts of Matabeleland and the central region. What complicated the matter even further was that people in Matabeleland and some parts of the Midlands voted overwhelmingly for ZAPU under Joshua Nkomo. In other words, the voters in Matabeleland and part of the Midlands rejected Robert Mugabe, a Shona-speaking leader. That meant the Ndebele speakers in Matabeleland and parts of the Midlands had rejected the new prime minister at the polls. Mugabe won in Shona-speaking constituencies but lost in Ndebele-speaking areas. Because Shona-speaking voters were in the majority, Mugabe won the majority of seats and became the leader of the country. With the majority of legislators behind him, Mugabe's party enacted laws that allowed the leader to use executive powers to sign whatever he wanted into law. Little wonder he constituted the Fifth Brigade to eliminate dissidents in Matabeleland and parts of the Midlands region.

When confusion with the dissidents escalated, the government considered steps to control the situation. Law enforcement was a slow way to arrest and bring the dissidents to justice. A more brutal approach was necessary to stop the enemy from overthrowing a democratically elected government. Justifiably, the state deployed the Shona-speaking Fifth Brigade to purge Matabeleland and parts of the Midlands of the undesirable elements.

The Fifth Brigade went to kill any civilian accused of sheltering and feeding the dissidents. There was no time to gather evidence about dissidents or anyone feeding the bandits. A report to the soldiers was enough to get swift justice done for the accused. A new problem arose as villagers started reporting whomever they hated in the community. The soldiers did not care. They killed anyone alleged to have interacted with dissidents.

The ongoing problems became so tribal that any Ndebele-speaking person, young or old, male or female, regardless of occupation, became the enemy of the state run by Shona-speaking people. Further communication breakdowns worsened the situation. The soldiers could not understand Ndebele, and the Ndebele-speaking villagers could not understand Shona. Since the soldiers had weapons, they harassed anyone who could not communicate in Shona. This became a replay of experiences with ZANLA cadres during the Guerilla War. At the height of the armed conflict, failure to speak Shona was defiance punishable by death. Only a few Ndebele-speaking locals who spoke Shona survived.

The killing of anyone accused of or reported to have collaborated with dissidents occurred in public. The victims had their hands tied to their backs, and were beaten, or were shot as a deterrent to others. Public humiliation would take place after rounding up the accused and ordering them to march to their deaths. In some cases, the soldiers kidnapped the accused and tortured them individually to death. The main targets were ZAPU officials and party supporters accused of sympathizing with dissidents. In other cases, the soldiers forced people to dig their own graves and buried them alive. A few people left for dead regained consciousness and lived with permanent injuries. Many years after the Fifth Brigade onslaught, countless people are permanently disfigured without help or hope for rehabilitation.

The soldiers screened everyone in Matabeleland and parts of the Midlands based on the language they spoke and the party they supported. If an individual spoke Shona, it was a foregone conclusion that the individual supported the Shona ruling party. There was no trouble for such a person. If the person spoke Ndebele, the assumption was that the individual automatically supported the opposition, ZAPU, and collaborated with dissidents. Conditions got so bad that all Ndebele-speaking people were labeled dissidents. The ultimate goal was to kill all dissidents, and that meant killing all Ndebele-speaking people.

Working for the government did not help as long as the employee carried a Ndebele last name or spoke the Ndebele language. The soldiers mounted roadblocks to harass, kidnap, and make the Ndebele-speaking people disappear without a trace. Easy targets for the Fifth Brigade were teachers who resided within school quarters and those who lived in the neighborhood. Teachers died for being influential in communities, for having the means to purchase food, and for traveling to commercial centers on paydays. Having money made the teachers suspicious.

The soldiers suspected that the teachers went to cities and towns to buy food for the dissidents. The other fear was that the teachers would go to urban centers to relay information to dissidents to help them avoid clashing with soldiers in the villages. When the teachers returned to school at the beginning of the week, they were harassed and accused of spying for dissidents. Many teachers lost their lives for going to the city, and others died for denying that they spied on the Fifth Brigade. Once framed by soldiers, the victims had no choice but to admit the accusation in the hope of forgiveness. Alas, the Fifth Brigade was not there to spare lives but to use every trick possible to make people confess and give a reason to butcher all who confessed.

The Fifth Brigade split into smaller units to be able to cover the targeted regions. The units had all the arms and services needed for war. These were well-trained units out to face an unknown number of dissidents. Despite the vastness of the units, the dissidents were elusive. The soldiers struggled to apprehend or kill the bandits. To save face, the soldiers turned to the defenseless civilians, accusing them of sheltering, feeding, and providing information to the dissidents to avoid the soldiers. They killed anyone as long as they spoke the Ndebele language. The killing styles were as different as the commanders'.

The small units did as they saw fit. The soldiers rounded up young men in villages and butchered them to death. In some cases, the men had their hands tied to their backs and were pushed into disused mine shafts. Many died from excruciating torture. The elderly men and women were set on fire in locked houses and burned to ashes. Women and girls were targets for rape and other forms of perversion. Pregnant women had their wombs slashed to view fetuses. Other women pulverized the unborn babies in a pestle and mortar, with blood splashing on those pounding.

The soldiers forced the Ndebele people to turn against each other. Parents beat their children to death. Children beat their parents to a pulp. Fathers and mothers slept with their children in the open to entertain the soldiers.

The soldiers were doing what the North Koreans trained them to do. They were out to kill the enemy. They were to be ruthless with the enemy and collaborators alike. If they could not find the enemy, they were to kill people who spoke the language of the enemy. They were to kill anyone who looked like the enemy. They were to kill anyone who fed the enemy. They were in the targeted regions to teach non-Shona speakers to accept the Shona-speaking prime minister, Robert Mugabe, as the legitimate leader of the country, not the Ndebele-minority leader of the opposition. The soldiers committed indescribable atrocities, leaving thousands of defenseless civilians dead. While the soldiers hunted fellow Blacks like animals, the international community remained silent.

The ruling elite, through the Fifth Brigade, wanted to annihilate the Ndebele-speaking people altogether. Then, the Shona-speaking people would manage the country as they pleased without competition from the Ndebele tribe. The majority tribe believed what the politicians were saying and hated the minority tribe for being a threat to their existence. It appeared as if atrocities were justified until some reasonable people within the ruling party condemned the killings. The reasonable men persuaded the ruling party to negotiate with the opposition to end the killings. The politicians from both parties came together and agreed to merge into a single organization with Robert Mugabe as the leader. Only then did killings stop, ending cries of distress. Only then did the Fifth Brigade units operating in Matabeleland and parts of the Midlands return to the barracks. Only then did Ndebele-speaking people find respite from the horrors of the Black soldiers deployed to obliterate the smaller Black tribe.

Chapter 3
Capture

A teacher named Zenzo, shortened to *Zee,* endured untold misery at the hands of the Fifth Brigade, specially deployed to crush the dissidents in Matabeleland and part of the Midlands. *Zenzo* is a name in the Ndebele language that translates to "performing outstanding work." Zenzo denotes being able to do extraordinary things, especially under difficult circumstances. Zenzo reflects work done supernaturally beyond human understanding. This is a name befitting miraculous survival in a difficult situation.

One Thursday morning in 1983, a unit of six Fifth Brigade soldiers invaded Kalaza Elementary School in the south of Matabeleland. Two soldiers were in front of the truck, and four sat at the back. The truck stopped at the school entrance, and the four soldiers at the back of the truck jumped out and held their guns in position. The two other soldiers in the front seat also got out of the vehicle and joined the four. The soldier on the passenger side led the unit and asked to speak to the head of the school. The driver remained at the entrance next to the vehicle. The other four stood at different points around the school.

When the soldiers arrived, the teachers and students were in assembly. At the gathering, the head was announcing plans for the week. The unit leader interrupted the gathering and ordered the teachers to guide the students to their classrooms. The teachers obliged and led the students to their respective rooms. The unit leader went to the office with the head of the school while the other soldiers ordered the teachers and students to hurry up. The soldiers spoke in loud tones and sounded incensed. The situation tensed up, and Zee sensed trouble in his 4th-grade class.

Within moments, the head of the school and the unit leader walked out of the school office and headed straight to Zee's classroom. The school head asked Zee to step out of the class. Immediately, the unit leader asked if he was Zee and he confirmed that he was. At that point, the lead soldier asked Zee to join him at the truck at the gate. Zee agreed but went back to the classroom to collect his jacket before joining the lead soldier to the truck. He scanned around the classroom and saw fear in the students' eyes. Anxiety gripped Zee as well. He wondered what the lead soldier had discussed with the head of the school. He could not understand what was wrong or why they were going to the truck. Meanwhile, the other four soldiers moved closer to Zee's class with guns drawn. As Zee returned to the door, the head urged Zee to cooperate with the soldiers to avoid trouble. He agreed and headed to the truck with the soldiers.

Zee could not understand what the inquiry was about. The soldiers asked him if he had seen dissidents and if dissidents had come to his home the previous night. Zee informed the soldiers that he had not seen dissidents, and that no such people had come to his home. His answers infuriated the soldiers, and they ordered Zee to jump into the truck and lead them to his home. Zee reminded the soldiers that he was at work and could not leave his students without supervision. He had answered the questions, and what else did the soldiers want to discuss? The soldiers would listen to none of his rationalizations and asked him into the truck. It became clear that the soldiers were up to something bad.

The driver who was waiting at the gate started the engine. Courage surged in Zee, and he asked where they were taking him. The lead soldier made it clear that Zee had questions to answer. He further inquired why he could not answer the questions outside his classroom before his departure. The lead soldier angrily told him to be quiet and wait until they arrived at his home. Reluctantly, Zee hopped into the truck, and they drove off to Zee's home.

The soldiers had driven past his home earlier on their way to the school. They could have planted incriminating evidence to justify their actions. Luckily, they did not break into any of the rooms. Little did Zee know that the soldiers had identified his home prior to coming for him at work. There was no way Zee could misdirect the soldiers to his home.

The six-kilometer journey between the school and his home took a long time and was bumpy. Close to his home, courage built up. It became clear that death awaited him. The ride was an opportunity to view passing nature as he prepared for his transition to the next life. There was nothing to say. Jumping off a moving vehicle was unwise: it would only complicate the situation. What was there to flee when death was beckoning? It would be a matter of time before the soldiers struck and killed him. The only way out was to toughen up and find a creative way to save his life.

Someone in the community had informed the soldiers that dissidents had been to Zee's home. That implied that he had fed the dissidents and not reported the event to the soldiers. It was an unpardonable crime to feed dissidents and not alert the soldiers. Collaborating with dissidents and concealing the information was open subversion and clear support for the enemy, punishable by death. It was for that reason that the soldiers pounced on Zee early in the morning at work.

The truth is that Zee had not entertained or fed dissidents the previous night. He had not seen dissidents, and he had not fed dissidents the day before or ever. The information that the soldiers had was wrong. The information was possibly from someone with a sinister motive. He had gone to bed early the previous night, and no unknown person had visited his homestead. The allegation that the soldiers were presenting to him was mischievous and false. He denied the accusation, and that infuriated the soldiers.

When they arrived, the soldiers who guarded him jumped out first, pulled Zee out of the vehicle, and immediately demanded to search his home. The captors searched all the rooms. If Zee had committed a crime, where was law enforcement to arrest and charge him with a crime? Why were the soldiers asking him about dissidents he did not see and feed? Had the soldiers assumed the dual responsibility of arresting criminals and defending the motherland? Those questions flooded Zee's mind as the soldiers moved from one room to the next in search of evidence to prove that Zee had fed the dissidents. What a waste of time and a futile exercise of authority! No dissident had passed through Zee's home, and he had not fed any dissidents.

In one room, they found an open 10-kg bag of cornmeal. The soldiers got excited that they had found cornmeal, likely used to cook for dissidents. The soldiers shouted, "You have cornmeal to feed dissidents." In his defense, Zee argued that he had children and that cornmeal was food for his children, not dissidents.

The soldiers seized the bag as evidence and put it in the truck. He argued that such a small portion of cornmeal could not feed dissidents. The soldiers did not pay attention to what the accused was saying. They had found something to use against Zee. Seeing that the soldiers could not understand, he decided to speak in English. The soldiers heard what he said in English but struggled to respond in the queen's language. At that point, the abuse started, and they slapped Zee for showing off his education. They ridiculed him and questioned if English would save his life by feeding dissidents who were against the state.

As they searched his bedroom, Zee got a warmer jacket, warm socks, and shoes in preparation for the unknown. They asked him once again if he had fed dissidents, and Zee maintained his innocence. He even asked why they were seizing children's food, and the reply was, "You must starve with the dissidents." It became clear that the soldiers' mission was to starve people and eliminate anyone suspected of collaborating with dissidents.

The soldiers persisted with their accusations. Someone had given them information, and they had found a bag of cornmeal. That was all the evidence they needed to charge Zee with a crime. To the soldiers, Zee was an enemy of the state for feeding dissidents. His sentence was death. A flashback to the Guerilla War reminded him of the cadres eliminating anyone envied, hated, or accused of being a sellout in the community. Here, he was now the culprit, envied, hated, and accused of a crime he did not commit.

Whoever betrayed him and the motive remain mysteries. It is unclear if his income, assets, or influence in the community threatened his enemies in the neighborhood. The treachery indicated that someone hated him and wanted him dead. The soldiers did not care about the motive for revealing his name. The marauding soldiers wanted traitors like Zee killed in public as a deterrent to other would-be dissident collaborators. This was a shocking and confusing accusation for Zee and his family.

No explanation could absolve the accused. Death was the inevitable sentence without appeal. There was no due process for Zee to present his side of the story. According to the soldiers, he had committed a crime against the state and had to die. Defense in Ndebele was useless, as the soldiers did not understand his language. The soldiers spoke Shona, which he did not understand. At the same time, the soldiers struggled to speak English, and communication completely broke down. When the soldiers completed their search, they formally charged Zee with the crime of feeding dissidents and failing to report the presence of dissidents to the authorities. The soldiers handcuffed him and pushed him into the truck for interrogation at the torture site.

Interrogation

From his home, the soldiers drove with Zee to Kozt Business Center, about 15 kilometers north of Kalaza. At the business center, the soldiers drank alcohol while Zee remained bundled in the open truck. After an hour, the soldiers came back to the truck and drove to Silobi Camp, another ten kilometers or so north for questioning. Silobi lies in the southwestern part of the Matopo Hills, south of Bulawayo City. Silobi Camp was central for detainees gathered from Matopo, Esigodini, and Gwanda districts. At the camp, men were stripped naked, enduring brutal torture, and inhuman interrogation. The sight of humans being treated like animals was devastating.

Many questions started racing through Zee's mind as he acclimatized to the camp filled with other Ndebele-speaking men. What he saw at the camp was barbaric, to say the least. What was even more heartbreaking was to see young men about his sons' age ready for slaughter, deprived of a chance to discover their purpose on earth. Black soldiers were about to end the lives of fellow Blacks who spoke a different language from the soldiers.

The young soldiers had the power and guns to do as they pleased with defenseless souls. The young soldiers were arrogant, abusive, and disrespectful. Even the parents who bore them would have been ashamed of the soldiers for behaving as they did, if not worse than animals. "Did their parents know what these young men were doing on duty?" "How would the parents feel when they saw the children they raised turn into such savages?" These were the disturbing thoughts that bombarded Zee as he watched the brutality play out before his eyes. Which parent, in his or her normal senses, would take pride in a child who went about butchering defenseless human beings as these young soldiers were doing? Who knew what these young men were doing and what was driving the young soldiers to act the way they did? These and other questions convinced Zee that expecting mercy from such beasts was a waste of time. Waiting sheepishly to hear screams fade as men drew their last breaths prepared him for his end. He also reasoned that fleeing would lead to the same fate: death. At that point, he felt motivated to flee at the slightest chance possible.

The problem with fear is that it tends to cripple reason. Given that the detainees outnumbered the soldiers, why they would tolerate abuse and torture without revolt remained inexplicable. He wondered why former ZPRA-trained guerillas would tolerate such abuse. He could not understand why the detainees with military skills would not seize the guns, overpower the few soldiers, kill them, and flee. The Silobi torture camp was far from urban centers with reinforcements. Why would the detainees with military training not organize other detainees to overrun the camp? The detainees could have easily outnumbered the soldiers and used arms to attack them and free other people held captive. There is no doubt that the soldiers would have shot some people, but the sheer number of detainees could have overpowered the few soldiers.

There was no need to wait obediently for the soldiers to kill the men one after another. It was clear that these soldiers had a plan to eliminate people in the camp based on how they treated those questioned. No wonder there was a rule at the camp that prisoners should not talk to each other for fear of revolt. Nevertheless, the deafening silence engulfing the camp and the fear of death knitted the detainees together without a word. The detainees might have died without knowing the next person, where they came from, or the crime they committed, but something made them feel that they had a common identity. They were Ndebele-speaking, all accused of collaborating with dissidents; no wonder they were dying together.

Getting away from the detention camp alive was the way out of pain, rather than seeking sympathy from the inhumane soldiers.

His turn for interrogation came. Like other detainees ahead of him, the soldiers asked him to strip naked and squat in line. The detainee ahead of him fell unconscious, and a soldier pulled him to the side to make way for Zee. One other soldier attached electric wires to Zee's private parts and began asking questions. When he responded with unacceptable answers, the second soldier turned on the power and administered an electric shock to the private parts. When turned on, the current threw Zee against some rocks, causing him to crush his back. The soldiers repeated the torture several times until he passed out. Like other detainees, Zee begged for mercy and professed innocence, but the soldiers were unrelenting, determined to break him.

The questioning took a harrowing hour or so, and the pain in the private parts was excruciating. At some point, his private parts were numb, and he wondered if he would ever use them again. Abuse and threats accompanied the torture, but the detainees never fought back but pleaded for sympathy, which never came.

Some people died during torture, but the ruthlessness continued unabated. Strangely, some police officers who visited the camp during the interrogation questioned why soldiers were torturing detainees, but none of the soldiers provided an explanation. Rather, the soldiers laughed and continued to have fun torturing the defenseless. After long spells of torture, the soldiers took a break, leaving Zee unconscious.

Chapter 4
Escape

Torturing the detainees was hard work for the soldiers. There were many people killed, piled up, and loaded into army trucks. The soldiers did most of the work and forced the remaining detainees to help load dead bodies into trucks. Zee watched in disbelief as the heap of dead bodies rose higher and higher before his turn. When called for interrogation, he went in with the hope that he would survive in order to flee. As noted earlier, his torture left him unconscious for some time. When he regained consciousness, he noticed that he was near his clothes, still naked.

The torture camp was quiet, with groups of detainees awaiting interrogation. The only noise around the camp came from the soldiers, who were playing soccer at a nearby field. The soldiers were taking a break after torturing and killing their prey. Soccer became entertainment and relief from butchering defenseless souls. The play carried on until it was almost dark.

The detainees who had been beaten and tortured were too weak to fight or sneak away. They waited for whatever the soldiers chose to do. Just then, it dawned on Zee that he should flee while the soldiers played. It was clear that if the soldiers found that he had regained consciousness, they would finish him off. Zee decided to take advantage of the dark and rocky terrain behind the camp to run away. He pulled on his clothes and dressed up. He quickly put on his shoes and lay flat for a few minutes while monitoring the soldier's movement. He looked around to figure out how to drag his body behind the rocks and vanish. He crawled stealthily backward and got behind the chain of rocks scattered about a meter from him. He was convinced that the rocks would shield him and block his view from anyone on the other side facing the camp.

Gazing at the detainees, he saw some individuals use hand signals to encourage him to sneak away. Taking one more gaze, he pulled his body slowly toward a chain of big, high rocks close by and squatted quietly for a few moments. He could hear the soldiers calling for the ball and screaming when the teams scored. The moment had come to move.

Zee fled behind the neatly woven rocks stretching a long distance toward the south. The chain of rocks connected to the Matopo Hills. He was at home in the Matopo Hills, having climbed and herded cattle there as a teenager. He knew that if he ran away far enough at night, he would hide where he played as a young man. What encouraged him even more was that the soldiers had more people to worry about at the camp than pursuing him alone. He was not such a threat that the soldier would abandon the camp just to look for him alone. Besides, the soldiers would avoid the hills in case the enemy hid there to attack. The rocks and hills gave him cover, allowing him to look ahead and walk fast. He weaved through the hills and avoided dirt to ensure that he left no footprints for the soldiers to track in pursuit. He picked up his pace and covered as much distance as he could to get away from the captors.

While it was exciting to sneak away from hell in the detention camp, a persistent fear in his mind was the possibility of an accident in the dark where he would get stuck between rocks. Such an accident would slow his movement, and he would likely be caught. He knew the soldiers would skin him alive if they caught him. Therefore, to avoid such an accident, Zee chose to work with the hills and the dark to take him as far away from the soldiers as he could. As expected, as it got darker, he knocked himself against rocks and fell several times, but picked himself up and continued moving. He thus chose to walk toward the foot of the hills, where there were fewer rocks and grass. It felt a little safer, and he picked up speed again.

As he walked, he felt sorry for the detainees who chose not to flee, knowing the soldiers would come back and kill them anyway. Yes, if he had been in their position and had been so tortured that he could not walk, he too would have sat and waited for death. There was little to do to help those he left behind, but focus on his escape.

The further he moved away from the torture camp, the quicker his fear dissipated. The hills suddenly provided the cover and security Zee needed. The hills provided protection as a mother nursed and comforted a child. His faith in the hills and the great power that resided in them reinforced his resolve to keep going. With no one to talk to, the hills and rocks whispered courage into his spirit, urging him to keep moving.

Negotiating his way through the hills the whole night to get away from the camp as far as he could became an adventure. As he moved further south toward his home, the hills and communal areas became more familiar. He even remembered the names of some of the people who lived near the hills where he was passing. Out of caution, he avoided coming into contact with anyone. He did not want to meet anyone lest people talk, and word got out about his movements, and the soldiers pursued him like an animal.

As planned, when he started running, his goal was to walk the whole night and find shelter in the hills close to his home. He would feel safer close to home without inviting trouble for his family. One way to keep soldiers away from his family was to find refuge at a location far from his neighborhood but accessible to his home. This would ensure that he avoided familiar faces who would report him to the soldiers.

In the dark, paranoia crept in, and some rocks appeared like people. Whenever rocks appeared to be standing like humans, casting shadows, Zee ducked for a few moments to see if the rocks moved. If there was no movement, he crawled forward and kept moving. Overall, hiding from shadows and falling slowed his movement, intensifying his fear and frustration. The journey through the treacherous terrain was long, and gradually, he became weary.

Fatigue increasingly took a toll on Zee, and optical illusions intensified his anxiety. Rocks and trees looked like human images, troubling Zee's mind as he maneuvered his way into darkness. Quickly, he decided to move away from the hills and rocks, drawing closer to the road. He made sure he walked on the grass along the road to conceal shoe marks in case the soldiers pursued him. He walked further south toward Gwanda Town. It was easier to walk on the road, and his pace improved. Whenever he heard the sound of a vehicle, he moved further away from the road and hid in ditches behind rocks and big trees. He proceeded through the thick bush close to the road until he was certain that there were no sounds along the road.

Thorns hooked themselves to his coat and pants, but he gently untangled himself to preserve the only clothes he had. There was a strong urge to rest, but he could not stop yet. He was going to walk until the early hours of the morning to get as far away from the torture site as possible. Although the urge to drink, eat, and get warm kept nagging, he dismissed the desires from his mind as he continued moving. He must have covered 30 kilometers on foot that night. At daybreak, he veered off the road and headed for the adjacent hills. He walked deep into the hills, where he found a cave and rested there.

The cave was clean and quiet, but dark. He could not see what lay at the back of the cave due to limited light. Close to the end of the cave lay a boulder with a flat surface. He climbed up the boulder to avoid creeping insects and wild animals that could be hiding at the back of the cave. Within a short time, while lying on his back, he fell into a deep sleep. He slept the greater part of the day and awoke toward the end of the day.

It was almost dark in the cave as rocks blocked the sun from entering. Disoriented, he sat up to recollect his senses and find his bearings. He could not understand why he was on an elevated boulder in a cave. Quickly, he remembered what was going on and why he found himself there.

Looking around the cave, bushman paintings engraved on the walls caught his attention. The paintings depicted hunters chasing, killing, and feasting on animals. The paintings also resonated with his experience as an animal hunted by soldiers. He, however, drew comfort from appreciating that his ancestors survived in the same cave, and in the same manner, he, too, would survive. Despite hunger and thirst, Zee remained in the cave until dark.

When darkness fell, he walked out of the cave and headed south along the road toward Kozt, where a friend and relative lived. Recall that Kozt is the place where Zee's captors stopped for a beer while he remained handcuffed in the truck after searching and confiscating a 10-kg bag of cornmeal from his home. After the drinks, the soldiers drove Zee to the torture camp, where he eventually escaped. Hiding at Kozt would be safer than hiding near his home. Very few people knew him, and he would feel comfortable near a friend and relative in the Kozt area.

Within a short distance from where he lodged for the night, he smelled ripe, sweet-smelling, yellowish-orange fruit called *umkhiwa*. The fruit derives its name from the yellowish-orange color of a white person's complexion. A white man is an *ikhiwa* in Ndebele. The tree was loaded with umkhiwa fruit, and he ate as much as he could. This was the first meal after a full day with nothing to eat. He was so excited and thankful for the meal after two nights without food. When content with fruit, he filled his pants as well as his inner and outer jacket pockets with the delicious fruit to save for later. He sat down and rested. After a while, he ate some more until he was full again. At that point, he felt thirsty, and the urge to drink drove him to keep moving to find water.

After walking for about thirty minutes, he saw a path deviating from the main road and heard cowbells along the path. He followed the path, and about 50 meters away, he found a well where cows were drinking. Like an animal, Zee bent to drink. He drank enough, washed his face, and quickly moved on in case people coming to fetch water and livestock saw him. It was safe to be paranoid and fearful of strangers to minimize false reports and rumors about him. The thought of soldiers apprehending him produced a paralyzing effect from head to toe. It was better to keep hiding like prey than be devoured by merciless predatory soldiers. His feet hurt, but he could not stop. He kept walking without feeling sorry for himself. His feet could hurt and blisters could develop, but being free from torture and false accusations was all that mattered at that point.

Full and hydrated, he walked the whole night. By daybreak, he had made it to the Kozt Hills. There, he explored the hills until he found a secure cave to rest for the day. At the cave, Zee would nurse injuries sustained from torture and falling along the way.

Chapter 5
In the Cave

The Matopo Hills are a marvel to the eye, stretching over miles with beauty beyond words. The hills stand out in a variety of shapes and offer deep valleys that are home to a variety of flora and fauna. Oral tradition reports that the Matopo Hills sheltered San hunters and local populations from predators moving past the hills. The same hills provided shelter to women and children during wars between the Ndebele warriors and the British imperialists seeking to colonize Matabeleland and gain control of the hills. The Matopo Hills were so scenic after the truce between the Ndebele warriors and the British explorers, the leading white explorer, Cecil John Rhodes, chose the Matopo Hills as his burial site. Rhodes' grave remains in the Matopo Hills to this day. No wonder anyone with an understanding of the value of the Matopo Hills would run to the hills for cover and refuge in tough times.

The Matopo Hills stretch and wind over a vast amount of land, about 70 miles to the south of Bulawayo, through the Dula and Kozt areas in the Gwanda-Esigodini region. Major rivers serving and interlocking with the hills include the Tuli, Mtsheleli, and Maleme. People hiding in Matopo hill caves draw water from the named rivers. Zee's ordeal forced him to flee torture and seek shelter in the Matopo Hills, like his predecessors during wars. He was convinced that he would survive in the hills, where ancestral protection dwelt.

The first cave Zee explored had cigarette stubs and was clearly unsafe. Other people had lodged there, and they could return at any time. He got away as quickly as he saw the evidence of human habitation. Moving further along and turning deeper, about half a kilometer north of the Kozt Hills, he found another unoccupied cave. He could see well to the end of the cave, and there were no wild animals, no crawling creatures, or any indication of human occupation. The cave, deeply concealed in the hills, looked safe, and Zee decided to lodge there for the night.

First Night

The cave was empty and warm. The hard rock, *amadwala* in Ndebele, closed the back of the cave, and other longer rocks were knitted on top to provide roofing. Crakes between the neatly woven rocks, amadwala, allowed a little draught to come into the cave and keep the interior of the cave cool. Sufficient light illuminated the cave, with the bulk of the light coming into the cave through the open front entrance. Dirt spread around the cave to provide a floor from the entrance to the back. Footprints and markings from various creatures could easily show on the soil. The cave was a complete room.

The temperature in the cave was comfortable for a person without blankets. No animal droppings were visible, which gave Zee hope that there would be no animals to fight for the cave. There were no snake trails or any other creeping insects.

Looking outside the cave, Zee picked five stones that he set at the entrance of the cave for defense. Using his bare hands, he pulled off a branch of a tree shaped like a cane. That cane became an additional tool for defense in the event a hungry animal or person attacked him.

The defense weapons, consisting of five stones and an improvised cane from a tree branch, gave Zee confidence to occupy and protect the cave. He returned to the back cave and identified a suitable position to lie down and sleep. He visualized where to line up the stones and the cane for defense when the need arose.

About a kilometer from the cave was the Tuli River, and Zee had access to water. The Tuli River had running water throughout the year. Rarely did its water dry up for people to dig wells. Running water was what he needed to drink, bathe, and wash his clothes. If he dug for water, other people would question who dug the well and follow his footprints to the cave. He avoided contact with members of the community lest reports go out about his presence in the area and soldiers track him. In the newly found cave, Zee had discovered a home. The cave was strategic, with qualities he needed for survival.

Re-arranging the cave took time, and toward the end of the day, Zee sat down to eat. He pulled out the umkhiwa fruit packed in his trouser pockets. Starting with the contents in the left pocket, he consumed the sweet fruit until full. A handful of pieces of umkhiwa remained in the left pocket. The fruit in other pockets, including the coat, remained untouched for future servings. Darkness fell, and within a short time, Zee fell asleep at the selected spot.

It was frightening to be in the dark alone, but Zee had no choice. He endured. The cave was a better place than the camp he fled. He entertained positive thoughts to strengthen the mind and prepare for the challenges ahead. Joy sprang up from within, and he thanked his maker for allowing him to escape from the soldiers who were planning to kill him slowly and painfully. He was grateful to find such a comfortable and safe shelter.

Darkness in the cave ceased to be fearful as the night progressed but became a divine medium to elude the soldiers, whose mission was to bring his tribe to extinction. He dozed off. The cave remained warm throughout the night from the heat absorbed by the rocks during the day. Zee slept peacefully throughout the night until the next morning.

A new day broke, and Zee was grateful to be alive and safe. He stood up, stretched his body, and moved around his new home. There was nothing frightening around the cave, and there were no suspicious marks or movements in the cave. He peered outside and saw the hills, the vegetation, and the cows grazing around. Those creations, though non-verbal, had become an inseparable part of his life.

The defensive tools were in the same place he laid them when he went to bed. The rough edges of the cane he hurriedly cut off before nightfall caught his attention. He realized that with rock around him, he could polish the edges of the cane and shape the cane into "induku," the smooth, creative design of the Ndebele defense weapon. Shaping the cane became work for the day.

The stone edges around the cave were effective at peeling off bumps along the handle. The handle had to be smooth to allow for a firm, adjustable grip when used. He rubbed the handle against the edges of the surface where he lay until the handle was smooth. By noon, he felt hungry and took a break to eat.

He continued with the fruit remaining in the left pocket and moved to the right pocket. He was full in no time and saved the rest of the fruit for future meals. He piled up the fruit seeds and threw them away far from the cave on his way to drink water in the dark. That was to ensure that the smell of umkhiwa fruit did not attract people, animals, or creepy creatures to the cave.

The cane-shaping assignment continued after the meal. The task involved removing the rough edges from the head of the cane. Carefully, he rubbed the rough edges against rock surfaces from different angles. He rubbed the cane's head against the rock to the left, to the right, and straight down. Little by little, a ball shape formed, and the cane was complete and ready for use. The cane had assumed full shape, with a smooth handle and a round head hard enough to hit and repel an attack.

Armed with the cane, Zee could venture out to find water at the Tuli River without fear. He waited until dark to walk to the river, ensuring that no one saw him. He found a pool with trees and reeds and bent over to drink like a cow. He drank enough and washed his clothes with his bare hands. He hung the clothes on bushes to dry. While the clothes were drying, he washed his body. Since he had no towel, he sat on rocks by the pool to dry and waited for the clothes to dry up as well. He enjoyed listening to creatures in the water move around the pool, and after a while, he put on his damp clothes, gulped more water, and headed back to the cave for the night.

Self-awareness

On returning to the cave, Zee followed the routine of the first day. He checked for intrusions and held his cane tight in case an animal had sneaked into the cave during his absence. Convinced that nothing had invaded his territory, he went back to his sleeping spot. It was warm in the cave after a cold bath. He lay there and struggled to sleep on his damp clothes. He could not remove the clothes lest something forced him to run from the cave. His mind started wandering.

Zee pondered on many things. He wondered how long he would live like that. He wondered whether the soldiers would stop hunting him down and when they would stop. He thought about the person who betrayed him to the soldiers and whether that individual would confess one day. He wondered if conditions in the country would ever normalize enough to allow him to return home and gather his family. His mind went all over the place until he was mentally exhausted. Suddenly, he fell into a deep sleep until a strange sound awoke him. He could not tell what the noise was, but the noise stopped after a few moments. Though shaken, Zee was ready to fight, yet nothing came to the cave. Sleep quickly overtook him again until the next morning.

Anxiety continued the next morning when it looked certain that life in the cave would continue for an unknown length of time. Zee thought about food, particularly where he could get daily sustenance apart from wild fruit. "Where would I get a change of clothes?" he thought to himself. What if the clothes got tattered and torn? What would he do? If people saw him in a pathetic state, they would assume that he was mentally challenged and not take him seriously. A few people, if any, listen to a man with torn clothes. Worse still, people would talk about him, and the information would likely reach the soldiers, creating more problems. It was safer to stay in the cave and avoid contact with other people altogether.

His appearance was deteriorating too. The beard was getting longer, and he wondered how he would look with an uncut beard if the hardship persisted. If people saw him in torn clothes with an unkempt beard, he would be a spectacle. Looking scruffy would make him appear insane, a creature to ignore. He recalled that people have little sympathy for the homeless and mentally disturbed and would blame the victims for their misery. He would not know how to present his case to people close to the cave. After all, the villagers were working hard to keep strangers out of their villages. Misfits attracted soldiers to the villages, and the soldiers ended up killing those who fed strangers.

Living like an animal in the cave, he would continue until a miracle occurred. He even wondered what the miracle would look like. What would happen? How would he respond to the miracle? Would he cry, laugh in disbelief, or run again? Those and other thoughts tormented Zee for as long as he was hiding.

Before long, self-pity crept in as questions mounted without answers. The situation remained the same day after day. He was stuck in the cave alone, with little hope of returning to a normal life. He soon realized that he alone was responsible for his thoughts. He needed a positive mindset, tough skin, and a strong will to face the ordeal. Only he alone could encourage himself to keep going forward.

Encouragement would only come from his mind. That meant thinking right, believing right, and acting right. As long as there were no external sounds, or movements of animals or intruders, inner thoughts were his only companion. "Why not pray in silence?" he thought to himself. He could use the silence in the cave to communicate with his creator.

Zee had all the time in the cave to commune with the maker. He had time to ask questions about why he was in a cave living like an animal and how he successfully escaped from the torture camp. There were many times when he expressed gratitude to the maker for being alive, albeit in a cave. Gradually, self-pity led to self-awareness.

Zee realized that he was not alone but in the presence of a silent power that had taken him out of danger to safety in the cave. He realized he had no means to rescue himself from the soldiers' wrath. He looked beyond himself and understood the reason for being in a cave alone. Such thoughts calmed his mind, and he appreciated the cave as his home. He felt peace fill the cave. There was comfort in the cave that he could not explain. For as long as he talked to the unseen being, he felt secure in his hiding place. When he entertained tormenting thoughts, the fear returned. The answer was to maintain contact with the power he could not see but sense. He felt protected in the cave and when he stepped out of the cave.

At the same time, the fruit was quickly running out. Inevitably, he had to find food to survive in the cave. In silence, he asked for directions to the right home with the right people who could understand his plight and provide food. As he listened for the right prompting, paralyzing questions bombarded his mind, but he remembered to be silent and wait. Just then, the thought of a friend and relative in the area crossed his mind. He knew that he had found an answer and waited for the sun to set to visit his friend and relative. Full of hope, Zee left the cave and headed toward the relative's home.

Asking for Food

He walked out of the cave and approached the relative's home he knew in the Kozt area. As he approached, his friend and relative rose to meet him. Yes, it was Joe, his friend and relative. Joe was shocked to see him alive after hearing stories of his capture and death at the hands of soldiers.

Hurriedly, Joe took Zee to the guest room, away from his family. The two men had last met a few years ago, but they knew each other well enough to keep a secret. He and Joe were distant relatives and had herded cattle together as teenagers; the reunion rekindled an old friendship.

Joe was a traditional leader and intercessor in the community. Members of the community confided in him and consulted him for rituals and other traditional practices. As a traditional leader, he listened to people's problems and communicated with ancestors for intervention. As a result, Joe kept people's secrets. Here was Zee in a situation seeking ancestral intervention. Zee was convinced Joe would keep his secret too.

Joe narrated stories he heard about Zee's disappearance and empathized with Zee for the experience. In turn, Zee poured his heart out and shared details about his experience. It was clear that Zee's situation was complex and needed divine intervention. In addition, both Zee and Joe agreed that the cave was the safest place to hide. They further agreed to keep Zee's situation a secret. Joe would be the only person to know about the cave.

Talking to a fellow human being was gratifying. Zee enjoyed listening to Joe talk. It was even more comforting to hear Joe offer support for the ongoing predicament. Zee had found the compassion that he longed for after his abduction. That was a complete shift from the inhumane treatment by the soldiers at the torture camp.

As they talked and reconnected, Joe's wife prepared a meal. After a while, Joe's wife, Bongi, came into the room with food. She presented a complete, warm portion of cornmeal, beef stew, and green vegetables. The food smell was inviting, and the sight was beyond anything he had seen or imagined in weeks. Zee added some hot peppers to the food to enhance the taste. The hungry man ate a large portion and cleaned up everything on the plate. The meal was a feast for Zee after going for days without decent food, except fruit.

Joe became the Good Samaritan, willing to walk with Zee through the unknown journey and provide sustenance. They hoped for safety one day at a time. After the meal, Joe offered Zee three blankets to take back to the cave. Joe opened the door to let Zee out, and once out, Zee led the way to the cave. Joe followed Zee until they disappeared into the rocks of the cave.

Chapter 6
The Inexplicable

While relaxing in the cave, Zee and Joe talked widely and covered various topics before parting for the night. The conversation created an opportunity for Zee to inquire about the whereabouts of soldiers, the curfew, and the prospects for a truce. There was no need to find out about dissidents because they were the state's creation. Ordinary people did not see dissidents in villages, but soldiers fabricated the existence of the marauding thugs to justify killing able-bodied individuals in the region.

Even more disturbing was the number of teachers who were genuinely serving children but had their lives cut short on spurious grounds. It hurt that a whole generation of children would go without proper education due to forced teacher disappearances. Teachers died in large numbers for being influential in communities and for making students aware of the Fifth Brigade's agenda in the region.

During subsequent visits, Joe brought food and water and provided updates about the situation in the country. Joe's visits made the cave feel like home. The visits gave Joe a chance to share news about everything and nothing in particular. The interaction brought hope and normalcy to the cave each time Joe visited. Joe's visits enabled Zee to keep track of the days of the week and holidays, including deaths in the community and around the country. Joe's visits continued under the cover of darkness for as long as Zee was hiding. After meals, Joe collected the dishes and took them back home for cleaning in preparation for the next meal.

Upon departure, Zee would reflect on the latest news and imagine the day he would return home to find out things for himself. He was grateful that he remained well for the greater part of his stay in the cave. There was never a day when he groaned with pain except for injuries sustained from torture, especially his back. He would feel residual pain in his back, especially during the cold season. Overall, he remained fit and had a sound mind to engage in deep conversations with Joe at meal times.

All alone, silent positive thoughts helped him cope with anxiety and a wandering mind. The voice he heard within was so reassuring and peaceful that he continually listened as if he were paying attention to another person. As a result of the connection he had with his maker and Joe, he found the peace he needed to cope with life in the cave day by day. Eventually, fading clothes ceased to be a problem. A growing beard became normal, and he stopped paying attention to it. As long as he bathed and had food, he was content and secure.

Rituals

Joe was surprised that Zee had chosen a cave that was near a site where he performed rain rituals. Zee's cave was also at Kozt Hills, about two kilometers away from Joe's cave. In his cave, Joe prayed for rain from the deity believed to reside in the hills. Every year before the rainy season, Joe would go to the cave to perform rituals. Joe's practices gave Zee a sense of security, knowing that he was in the presence of a power that cared for people and provided rain.

While Joe performed rituals and interceded for the community, Zee was also growing spiritually in the cave. Uncertainty and pain were pushing Zee away from self-pity as hope pulled him closer to the deity for protection. Each time he prayed, his mind calmed down, and peace fell on him. He would sleep while praying and rest well for the night. Continual prayer led to unexplainable occurrences that revealed the presence of a power greater than he knew.

Strange Occurrences

After one year in the cave, strange things started happening. Loud drumbeats sounded every night as if there were *ukuthethela* ceremonies. Ukuthethela is the Ndebele ceremony of appeasing ancestral spirits to restore order one year after the death of an adult. The ukuthethela ceremony takes place during difficult times. The belief is that when there is turmoil in the family, the deceased adult's spirit is unsettled, and the living must do something to help the departed spirit settle in the next life. It is a long-held belief among Ndebele-speaking people that the spirits of the dead look after and direct the lives of the living. That means when things go wrong in the present life, there is turbulence in the spirit world. The living must appease the spirit of the deceased to restore order in the physical world. Since Zee was in a difficult situation, it was likely that the spirit of one of the deceased elders was upset and calling for attention through Zee's predicament. The enactment of ukuthethela was, therefore, necessary to restore normalcy in Zee's life.

The drumbeats signified that something was happening in the spirit world. Whatever was going on, Zee reverently kept silent in the cave and respected the process. "Who would beat drums so loud and so late at night?" "Were there people on the mountain performing rituals?" These were puzzling questions that remained unanswered.

Sounds interrupted Zee's sleep. He feared that people in the community visited caves around the hills and would eventually come to his cave to perform various rituals. If people found out that Zee was hiding in one of the caves, word would spread to the soldiers, and the killers would come to hunt him down and end his life. The drumbeats continued for several months until Zee accepted the sound as normal. He was not even curious to look out of the cave to see who was playing the drums or why. The drumbeats remained a total mystery.

Great Grandmother Appears

One afternoon, drums sounded louder. The sound drew closer to the entrance of his cave. That was scary, as he feared that human beings were beating drums and coming to the cave where he boarded. He thought of fleeing but restrained himself and decided to face whoever came. He kept his defense weapon close to him and waited as the sounds drew nearer. To his amazement, Zee's great-grandmother, Gogo MaTshuma, who died when Zee was in elementary school, appeared at the entrance of the cave. Zee was wide-awake and saw the event unfold before his own eyes. Gogo is grandmother in the Ndebele language, and great-grandmother is "khokho." When she was still alive, the family addressed her as "Gogo MaTshuma" rather than "Khokho MaTshuma." Gogo MaTshuma looked her very self, as Zee knew her. She was dressed in traditional dance attire: a black and white skirt with black, white, and red beads across her chest. She danced to the rhythm but avoided eye contact with Zee while dancing. Zee could not see anyone playing drums either. He was so overjoyed and terrified at the same time to see his great-grandmother, whom he loved and who played with him when he was young. When Zee looked at his great-grandmother, she smiled and danced away without saying a word. This was an enigma, leaving Zee stunned once again.

A Leopard Appears

One sunny afternoon, while talking to his maker during the second year in the cave, a leopard appeared and stood at the entrance of the cave. Zee sat still as the colorful animal stared at him. The leopard did not attack or move toward Zee but stood and looked at him. He looked back at the leopard, ready to strike if the leopard jumped to devour him for dinner. The gazing contest seemed to take forever, with the leopard at the entrance and Zee at the back of the cave. After an agonizing forty-five minutes to an hour, the leopard looked at him once more and left without a fight. It was as if the leopard was showing its presence as a protector, rather than a predator.

What a relief it was to see the leopard leave. Zee remained frozen in his spot even after the leopard's departure, for fear it would lay an ambush and spring back to attack. When dusk fell, Zee gained the courage to stand up and walk toward the entrance of the cave. Looking around and seeing no trace of the strange visitor, Zee stretched his body for a few moments and returned to his resting spot in disbelief. Whatever the meaning of the incident, it remained a mystery. The scary moment gave Zee a reason to be grateful for life. This was yet another event to demonstrate that he would survive whatever threatened his life. The leopard only appeared once and never came back during his entire stay in the cave.

The escape from the soldiers, finding a cave, the appearance of the deceased great-grandmother, and the imposing image of the leopard at the entrance of the cave all left Zee bewildered yet hopeful. Not even Joe could interpret the flow of events and provide a meaningful explanation for the strange occurrences. Both Zee and Joe agreed that the answer lay in drawing closer to the silent source of protection. Humbly, Zee continued to talk and listen to the silent presence in the cave while the soldiers wreaked havoc on communities.

Chapter 7
Journey Out

It takes half a day to walk from the Kozt Hills to the main ancestral Ndebele shrine at Njelele in the Matopo Hills range. A round trip on foot from Zee's cave in the Kozt area to Njelele and back takes the whole day. As a traditional healer specializing in rain rituals, Joe performed basic rituals at Kozt Hills, close to the cave where Zee hid. Occasionally, Joe took requests further to the Njelele Shrine, also believed to be where the deity resided. Traditional healers and spirit mediums like Joe approached the Njelele Shrine for additional consultation on intricate issues at difficult times. Joe found himself faced with Zee's complex problem, which he could not manage alone. Joe had no choice but to present Zee's problem to the deity at the Njelele Shrine.

One day, Joe suggested that Zee join him on a trip to the Njelele Shrine. That would be an opportunity for Joe to present Zee's case to the ancestors and the higher power at the Njelele. Zee agreed but made it clear to Joe that he had nothing to offer at the shrine. He had no money to buy food. He had no money to buy clothes. What he was wearing was all he had, with no replacement. In other words, he had no money to buy the provisions required at Njelele. He had nothing, yet he needed help. Joe understood Zee's predicament and assured Zee that he would help. Then, preparations for the trip began.

Joe purchased all the provisions for the Njelele rituals, including linen to kneel on, snuff to sprinkle on the ground during the rite, and traditional brew to pour on the ground as a libation to the ancestors. Joe and Zee agreed on a date of departure and planned the journey. They were fully aware of the risks likely to arise during the trip. There was a possibility of meeting other villagers who knew Joe, increasing the likelihood of spreading the information to the soldiers. Zee thought, "News and rumors spread fast if people see a strange-looking man in the neighborhood." Indeed, Zee looked strange with long hair, a long beard, and fading clothes. His appearance would catch people's attention unless they devised a plan to make Zee look ordinary.

The next day, Joe returned to the cave during the day to shave Zee's hair. Joe brought a gallon of water, a pair of scissors, a shaving stick, soap, and a pocket mirror. Anyone seeing Joe carry a gallon of water would have thought Joe was on a journey and needed water to drink. Little would anyone know that Zee would use the water to shave and improve his facial appearance!

Joe started by trimming Zee's hair with a pair of scissors. Next, Zee poured water on a rock to wash off the shaven beard and checked the shaving success through a pocket mirror. He followed by shaving his head clean. At that point, Joe returned home to give Zee a chance to prepare for the trip to the Njelele Shrine.

Since Zee had soap, he went to the river to wash his clothes. As usual, he drank, bathed, and hung his clothes on tree branches to dry. He would remain naked while he waited for the clothes to dry. He let the clothes dry for a little while lest a situation arise for him to run. As a result, he put the clothes on and walked back to the cave.

The other important step to think about in preparation for the journey was to avoid roads and paths. That was to keep away from other people who would likely talk about an unknown person in the neighborhood. Out of fear, people would conclude that the unfamiliar face was a dissident, bringing danger and death to Zee. To avoid people, Zee would walk through the bush at the foot of the hills until he crossed the main road. On the western side of the main road, there would be a path that passed by a big umkhiwa tree with two tall, dry branches pointing right. Zee would meet Joe by that umkhiwa tree. From the meeting point, they would follow a path and walk together toward the Njelele Shrine.

The arrangement was that if Joe got to the rendezvous before Zee, he would put a branch of a tree on the spot by the umkhiwa tree and relax close by. Joe would see Zee upon arrival. If Zee arrived at the spot earlier than Joe did and there was no branch on the spot, then Zee would put the branch of a tree at the meeting point and wait until Joe came.

On the appointed day, Zee left early in the morning, walking past the northern side of the Nathisa Business Center along the foot of the Matopo Hills. Rocks along the hills and trees of various sizes provided adequate cover from people wandering in the morning like Zee. The journey was safe and uneventful. Zee met no one and hoped no one saw him heading toward the meeting point. After all, the area had visitors from different parts of Matabeleland passing through on their way to the Njelele Shrine. Zee would not be the first person walking through the area. The concern was that people are unpredictable, and they could talk about anyone or anything they see. Zee chose to walk with confidence as if he knew the area.

Around noon, Zee arrived at the spot where he would meet Joe. When Zee arrived at the spot, there was no branch. That meant that Joe had not arrived. He put a branch under the big umkhiwa tree as planned and sat under a tree to see if anyone approached the spot. Zee relaxed in full view of the branch at the spot and looked in the direction of the hills. If anyone walked past the spot and saw the tree branch, it would mean nothing except for Joe and Zee.

Zee waited for about an hour before Joe arrived. At some point, Zee became anxious about Joe's delay. He did not want to wait too long until people passed by and saw him. Zee's worry was that if anyone saw him sitting under a tree for a long time, the individual would get suspicious and tell others. The strategy was to avoid contact with other people to minimize suspicion. Joe's delay became a concern.

When Zee was almost dozing off, a figure approached through the forest toward the spot. The individual was in dark clothes with a hat over his face, but he could not tell if it was Joe. Zee remained quiet until the person got to the spot. The individual looked around and removed his hat. The individual looked in Zee's direction. Just then, Zee coughed loud enough for the individual to hear. The person waved. It was Joe! Zee rose from where he was and approached Joe at the spot. It was a great relief to meet as planned.

Joe explained why he was late. He admitted that he was delayed at home, given that there were chores to complete before departure. He was not sure when they would return, and he put things in order in case they returned after more than a day. The reasons Joe gave for the delay made sense, and there was no need for an argument. Zee volunteered to carry the ceremonial package that Joe had removed from his back. Immediately, they proceeded together to the Njelele Shrine, with Joe leading the way.

It was a hot day, and the two friends faced the intense afternoon heat on their way. With Joe proving to be reliable, Zee hoped for a trouble-free journey and visualized success at the shrine. After all, Joe knew the area, and he purposely weaved through the bushes to avoid contact with other people on the way to the shrine. Zee and Joe rested under trees a couple of times, taking turns carrying the ceremonial package.

Shrine

Upon arrival at the Njelele Shrine, Joe and Zee reported to the custodian to seek permission to enter the shrine. They gave the reason for the visit and sat where they were directed to sit. They maintained reverence, as required of all who entered the shrine.

There, the custodian directed all activities in and out of the shrine. Those who knew the procedure, like Joe, helped the newcomers, like Zee. Frightening silence gripped the entrance of the shrine so that a falling stone would send people fleeing for cover. Zee feared the possibility of a stampede if people started running from whatever scared them. If there was pandemonium, there would be many injuries and deaths.

Joe had been to the shrine several times before, and he knew what to do. Zee followed Joe anxiously and did as advised. Zee was fearful of entering the dark side of the shrine to present the petition. The consolation was that the people who went in returned complete and looked vibrant. That gave Zee the assurance that he would come out alive and reenergized too. The only problem was that the process of moving toward the entrance was agonizingly slow. Nevertheless, they waited their turn after walking the long distance to get to the shrine.

Their turn to approach the sacred spot finally came. At that point, the custodian led Joe and Zee to the mediator. The mediator was a man endowed with the potential to communicate with the ancestral spirits and the deity. He facilitated the transfer of requests from worshippers like Zee through ancestors to the deity and back to the worshippers. The mediator, in turn, directed Joe and Zee to a specific point where they sat barefooted. Joe presented the ceremonial package, including paper money, to the mediator. In the bag were white linen unrolled to kneel on, snuff to sprinkle on the ground during the rite, and a traditional brew to offer the ancestors as a libation. At that point, they were ready for the ritual.

Joe and Zee introduced themselves to the deity and named the ancestors they recalled, male and female, one at a time. The focus then shifted to Zee. The custodian instructed Zee to sprinkle snuff on the linen and pour the traditional brew on the ground as he called out the ancestors' names. The moment Zee had been waiting for had come. He gladly complied, knowing he had direct contact with his deceased relatives. The next step was to present his predicament to his ancestors.

Joe took over the presentation and described Zee's plight. He asked Zee to repeat what to say to the ancestors. Within a few moments of following Joe's lead in speaking to the ancestors, courage built up in Zee, and he opened up and started speaking his heart out. After he poured out his heart about his predicament, Joe and the custodian interjected and asked him to add more detail or clarify some of the things he mentioned. Zee concurred, provided the missing details, and clarified what was vague. By speaking from his heart, Zee let out the pain bottled up inside. He cried. He whined. He spoke angrily until he calmed down, seeking to understand what was happening. He pleaded for protection and requested answers to the endless questions in his mind.

As Zee was pouring out his heart in the shrine, the mediator listened and conveyed the message from the deity back to Zee. The mediator discerned what the spirit was saying and assured Zee that his protection, safety, and success depended on his patience and wise judgment in his daily conduct. Whatever befell Zee after the visit to the shrine was on him. He was to pay attention to the silent voice and act on what he heard.

Joe and Zee thanked the greater power, the ancestors, for hearing their request and asked for protection on their way back home and thereafter. The mediator confirmed that the deity heard and would grant the request. The word from the shrine was comforting to Zee and Joe; they walked out feeling complete and motivated to return home without fear.

Return to the cave

Late in the afternoon, when consultation at the Njelele shrine ended, Joe and Zee put on their shoes and prepared to leave. As they exited the shrine, Joe looked at Zee, nodded his head a few times, smiled, and remarked, "We have done it." Zee smiled back and stretched his arm to shake Joe's hand in appreciation for his unwavering support. Zee was happy that he presented his predicament to the deity and felt accepted. Even more gratifying was that he received feedback from the deity with the clear instructions he needed to survive. For all the good that took place in the shrine, Zee could not thank Joe enough. Satisfied with what they had accomplished, they started heading back home.

On the way, Joe and Zee reflected on what transpired at the shrine. They talked about what they saw, the sounds they heard, and the instructions for Zee's survival. The darkness was so striking that they both agreed that something beyond their understanding dwelt there. The serenity that came from the darkness was so peaceful that fear ceased, making the guests comfortable in the shrine. The order in the shrine was also worth talking about. The movement from the entrance, including the transfer of guests from the custodian to the mediator, was well structured. The exchange of information between the guests and the deity flowed without confusion. They both observed that the guests presented different requests and received matching responses. While awaiting clearance to leave the shrine, Joe and Zee also noted that those who were in front of them received unique answers to their requests. No one received the feedback and guidance that Zee received. The instructions were specific and directed to Zee's unique situation, making communication with the deity genuine.

According to Zee, it was little wonder that thousands of people visited the shrine for guidance, cleansing, and many other reasons.

Strangely, the deity listened to every request presented and responded to suit each need. Responses given back to attendees were clear so that people could execute instructions to mitigate ongoing problems. It was humbling to receive the words and direct guidance from the deity. The response reflected the care and compassion of the highest order. To receive attention from a power that provided rain to the nation and immediate intervention was truly comforting to Zee. In humility, he would remain in continual prayer, fully convinced that the deity would keep him safely back in the cave.

The trip to the shrine was a necessary escape from the cave. The visit was an opportunity to view the rolling hills and appreciate a variety of rock shapes, patterns, and unique designs of trees interlocking to form the undulating horizon. Some rocks were shaped like human heads with arms joined together to provide cover. Strangely, some rocks stood like bare-breasted women, signifying provision to a helpless child like Zee under the circumstances. The rock shadows cast on the ground were like a multitude of warriors above, protecting the weak on the ground. Trees of varying sizes provided shade to protect citizens from the heat and block eyes spying from the hilltops. It was as if the trees and bushes walked with Zee and Joe, shielding the two men from curious eyes along the way.

Zee was relieved to breathe fresh air and walk through nature. There were comforting sounds of the wind blowing against the hills and through trees, reinforcing the connection with the surroundings. Under such beauty and connection with nature, never once did Zee think they could meet soldiers.

Zee and Joe walked together toward the big umkhiwa tree, where they initially met on their way to the shrine. They talked in low tones to avoid attracting people's attention. They came to a point where they exhausted the discussion on the internal dynamics of the shrine.

From there on, they talked about general stuff. They talked about rain, the planting season, and hope for a good harvest. As they approached villages, they maintained silence as they navigated their way to where they initially met.

In total silence and occasional sign language, the only sounds they heard were those of animals and shoes hitting the ground as the two men walked briskly. Eyes looked ahead, and minds processed different issues, but they could not voice out the thoughts for fear of arousing curiosity in the neighborhoods they walked past. Each time Zee and Joe looked at each other, their heads nodded in unison for encouragement to keep going. They walked without a break until they reached the meeting point by sunset.

At the rendezvous, they sat down and rested. They discussed a walking plan to take them back to their respective homes. Since it was getting dark, they would walk along the road and separate to avoid cars and people coming in their direction. After about an hour, with the moon rising beautifully, they started the last leg of the journey.

They walked side by side along the main road toward Joe's home. When the road wound around, they took a shortcut and connected with the road further along. No one and no car came their way. The only fear was meeting soldiers on foot. It was a tense eight-hour walk, arriving at Joe's home at dawn, hungry and exhausted.

Joe's wife, Bongi, woke up to make a fire and to start the tired men with tea for warmth. Hurriedly, Bongi presented the tea to the two men and left them to relax. Zee was so content with two cups of tea and bread that he felt sleepy. Thanking Joe and Bongi, Zee excused himself and headed back to the cave. The morning was breaking, and Zee could see his way to his refuge. Going through and under rocks, he made it to the cave.

It was dark in the cave, and Zee could hardly see what was inside. He became fearful, not knowing what was in the cave. The fatigue he was beginning to feel on his way to the cave disappeared when he faced darkness in the cave. Instead of panicking, he chose to sit at the entrance until the light shone into the cave. Before long, he could see into the cave. He looked around the cave for intruders. No wild animal had found its way into the cave while Zee was gone. He shook the blankets to blow away insects, and nothing fell out. Satisfied, he made his bed and sat down to wind down. Next, he thanked the deity for a safe trip to the shrine and back to the cave. He lay down, and within a few minutes, Zee was fast asleep. It was a good day's rest until early evening when Joe brought some food.

As usual, Zee and Joe talked over the meal. Joe reminded his friend to remain in constant prayer, as advised by the deity. Zee consented and thanked Joe for his help once again. After the meal, life in the cave continued with an uncertain end. Zee continued with daily devotions as a way of driving away bad thoughts and keeping himself focused on the good around him. The immediate call was to exercise judgment to avoid unnecessary trouble on a daily basis.

Chapter 8
Risky Adventures

During the third year of successful hiding, Joe asked Zee to visit his home for longer periods. This would take longer than a day at a time. Zee welcomed the gesture as a healthy break from the seclusion of the cave. Clearly, that would be an opportunity for Zee to relate to other human beings, hear the latest news, see crops growing in fields, and to gaze at animals feeding the young. Joe also needed a break from the monotony of taking food to the cave every night. At the same time, the curfew was still effective, and the two men were wary of surprise raids by the soldiers who were still looking for Zee. The visit would require careful planning and caution for Zee to sneak back into the cave if soldiers appeared. On the appointed day, and as tactfully as they always did to avoid strangers, Joe came to the cave to take Zee to his home.

A short distance away from the cave, as they walked through the thicket, they saw soldiers patrolling at a distance. Zee and Joe took cover under trees and hid, wondering what they had done to themselves. There was no one to blame but them for their poor timing. The soldiers did not see the two friends as they kept walking in the western direction. They remained in hiding until soldiers disappeared toward the outlying hills to the west. After a while, they heard the sound of a vehicle. It stopped where the soldiers headed along the road and sounded off again, heading north toward Bulawayo. Joe concluded that the vehicle had picked up the soldiers and driven off.

Zee was frightened to walk to Joe's home and chose rather to return to the cave. What if the soldiers did not go but remained in the area? What if they came to Joe's home and found him there? The questions caused such unbearable anxiety that Zee felt safer in the cave than risk capture again. He remembered the advice from the shrine that his safety depended on his judgment. After careful consideration, Zee chose to reschedule the visit to Joe's home for another day.

The following Saturday, Joe went on a reconnaissance mission, covering a radius of about five kilometers around his homestead. The purpose of the journey was to check if there were soldiers patrolling the area and talk to people about the soldiers' whereabouts. There were no soldiers, armed people, or villagers moving about along the way. The villagers avoided contact with the soldiers to avoid answering questions, harassment, and baseless arrests. As a result, villagers kept to their homes and only moved to fetch water, collect firewood, gather livestock, and go to the store.

After the mission, Joe proceeded to Zee's cave to persuade him to join him at his home. Zee recounted the previous experience that almost got him into trouble. Instead, Joe assured Zee that he had combed the area and that there were no soldiers or armed thugs roaming the area. Reluctantly, Zee agreed, and they left for Joe's home.

On his arrival at Joe's home late in the afternoon, he asked Zee how he was coping with loneliness in the cave. Zee narrated his strange experiences, such as the drumbeats, great-grandmother's appearance, and dance at the entrance of the cave, as well as the unexpected visit by a leopard. Joe marveled at the experiences with little to say. The truth was that Zee had adjusted well to seclusion and was reluctant to be away from the cave. Joe, in turn, presented his interpretation of the political situation, including the negotiations between the ruling party and the opposition aimed at finding a truce to end the killing of innocent civilians. The two friends spoke in low tones to avoid attracting other people to where they were seated.

Bongi, Joe's wife, also came to join them. Zee and Bongi talked to each other at close range for the first time.

Bongi told Zee where she grew up and when she came to live at the present location. She further expressed anger at the soldiers' cruelty in killing defenseless civilians. After a long chat with comforting laughter, Bongi left to prepare food.

For a start, she served hot tea with fresh cow milk in porcelain cups and saucers. Margarine and strawberry jam spread on bread accompanied the tea. Joe and Zee took their time to drink tea, joke, and enjoy each other's company. After downing a few cups of tea that Zee had not tasted in a long time, Joe collected the utensils and returned them to the kitchen, where his wife was preparing the main meal.

After a while, Bongi brought in the main meal. She served dried beef, potatoes, green vegetables, and rice. Zee enjoyed a complete, warm meal in a relaxed manner for the first time in a long time. Joe encouraged Zee to keep eating until he was full. By then, the sun had set. Once again, Joe collected the dishes and took them to his wife in the kitchen. When Joe returned, he invited Zee to another room, where he would relax for the night.

Bchind thc onc-roomcd grass, lodging next to Joe's big house, was a chain of rocks big enough to hide a man standing. In the guest room was modest furniture with a single bed, a chair to the side, and a wooden wardrobe at the foot of the bed. There were three neatly folded blankets positioned at the head of the bed. The room had two windows about a meter above the ground, big enough to let an adult out if the need to run arose. Alternatively, he could hide in the wardrobe if the situation demanded it. Joe thought hard about the room to prepare for a raid in case soldiers pounced. Both men knew that they were taking a risk, but the move was necessary for Zee's sanity.

Upon Joe's departure, Zee locked the door to prepare to sleep. He had a peaceful sleep until the early hours of the morning when the dogs started barking incessantly as if intruders were approaching. Zee awoke and dressed up, ready to act in case soldiers raided the homestead. He removed the key from the keyhole and stood by the wardrobe to ensure that no one looking through the keyhole or windows could see him. He got ready to open the closest window and slip away toward the rocks behind Joe's home if the need arose. He waited until the dogs stopped barking.

No sound competed with the dogs, and Zee could not guess what the dogs were barking at. When silence returned, Zee went back to bed with clothes on in case soldiers attacked. About an hour after the first barking, the dogs started howling again. This time, it was as if they were attacking something. Just then, a donkey sneezed, and Zee could tell that the dogs were fighting to drive away a donkey. After the confusion, he got tense and could not go back to sleep until the next day.

The next morning, Joe and Zee talked about the barking from the previous night. Zee narrated how ready he was to run, only to find that the dogs were barking at a donkey. Joe, for his part, peered through the window to see what was happening and relaxed when he saw the donkeys moving about. It was a tough night for Zee, and he chose not to have another tense night at Joe's place. By sundown, he decided to return to the cave to hide from everything. When they parted, Joe insisted that Zee should visit again when he felt like it.

Guest Room

On another occasion, toward the end of the third year of hiding, tired of loneliness in the cave, Zee chose to visit Joe at his homestead. He arrived when Joe was about to go to the field to drive away baboons. The baboons had a tendency to ravage corn. Joe quickly led Zee to the guest room he used the last time he visited and headed to the field. He reminded Zee that if the soldiers showed up, he would yell as if shouting at baboons. That would be a signal for Zee to sneak out. If Joe found baboons in the field and there were no soldiers, he would drive them out without making any noise. Zee could not join Joe out in the field lest villagers see him and soldiers come by. Rightly, Zee went into the guest room and made himself comfortable. Tempted by the sight of a bed with sheets on and feeling tired, Zee lay down.

Before he could doze off, Zee heard a noise coming from the field where Joe was. He stood up and peered through the window and to see soldiers talking to Joe. Zee froze with fear. He regretted visiting Joe. He wondered what had gone into him to think of visiting Joe on that particular day. "Could Joe be doing something behind his back?" he quivered. Under the circumstances, it was futile to debate whether Joe was a snitch or not. Joe had sent out a signal and spoken loudly for Zee to hear, as he had promised. The onus was on Zee to act to protect himself.

At that point, his safety lay in positioning himself in such a way that he would monitor the soldiers' movements and respond accordingly. If the soldiers headed to the homestead, Zee would confirm that Joe was snitching and get ready to sneak out and hide behind the rocks close to the room where he was. Once shielded by rocks, he would disappear into the hills and find his way back to the cave. He kept still and watched.

He saw the soldiers talk to Joe. After a little talk, Joe and the soldiers parted ways. Joe continued monitoring his field. The soldiers also moved away toward the west in the direction of the main road. Zee kept his gaze on the soldiers until they disappeared toward the road. Joe kept on moving around the field to prove to the soldiers that he was busy monitoring the field. He did not walk back home right away; only later did he return. When he returned, he did other things around the house without coming to where Zee was. It felt safe when Joe returned home, and Zee fell into a deep sleep until it was dark.

Without turning on the lights, Joe checked on Zee and found him awake. In low tones, Zee asked what the soldiers wanted. Joe explained that the soldiers were looking for dissidents in the area. He assured the soldiers that he had not seen any armed men near his home and that he was in the field to drive away baboons and not dissidents. Coincidentally, as Joe and the soldiers were conversing, baboons did show up, and Joe excused himself to drive the baboons away. It was then that the soldiers left to allow Joe to drive the baboons away. Joe took his time to drive the baboons away and explore the whole field, letting the soldiers walk away from his field without suspicion. When the conversation ended, Joe shut the door, leaving Zee alone in the room. It was a while before Joe returned with dinner.

For dinner, Zee had hot beef stew, green vegetables, and cornmeal. It was a pleasant feast and a celebration to thank the deity and all ancestors for diverting soldiers away from Joe's homestead. Joe hinted that the soldiers were out to track dissidents reported to have come in Joe's direction. The soldiers were satisfied with Joe's explanation and happy to find him busy in his field. To that end, the soldiers had no reason to search Joe's homestead but kept pursuing the dissidents further west.

Soldiers in military gear were symbols of cruelty that sent chills down Zee's spine. When he caught a glimpse of the soldiers, Zee was ready to spring into action and run for his life if the need arose. He would have run into the hills and disappeared from the heartless beings. From the house where he hid, he watched every move the soldiers made and was ready to flee if the soldiers came toward Joe's home. Clearly, he had used poor judgment and visited Joe on the wrong day. He would have avoided trouble by staying in the cave despite the solitude. After dinner, Zee departed and returned to the cave.

The anxiety of the day was so intense that Zee could not sleep over at Joe's place for the night. Sleeping at Joe's home would have been impossible, knowing that the soldiers were in the area. "What if they returned at night," was a line that kept spinning in his mind. The cave was safer for him and less risky for Joe and his family.

In the dark, he found his way to the cave. Peace welcomed him back from the scary moments he experienced at Joe's home. It was nerve-wracking to visit Joe during the day and unbearable at night. Zee regretted the danger he put Joe's family in by accommodating him. He did not want to lose Joe for his commitment to his welfare and safety. He did not want anything bad to happen to Joe's wife, for she was such a good cook and very compassionate. It was safer to hide and eat whatever Joe brought in the evenings than to risk visiting his friend.

Sneaking Home

As the third year ended, Zee allowed his mind to wander. He felt a strong urge to walk home and check on his family. He was weary of solitude and longed to see his wife, children, and animals. When Joe brought food in the evening, Zee shared his intention to leave the next day. Joe reminded Zee to use his judgment and be tactful during the adventure. As usual, after chatting the evening away, Joe collected the dishes and returned home. Without thinking carefully and developing a plan to dodge soldiers and villagers along the way, Zee made up his mind and rushed to action.

The next day, late in the afternoon, Zee set out. It would take him half a day's journey to walk home. The journey between the cave and his home was uneventful. He knew the way. He knew how to avoid villages as he navigated his way home. Accordingly, he met no soldiers or anyone else along the way.

He arrived home around midnight, and his dogs barked at him. He called their names, and they calmed down. His wife, Thembekile, or *Thembi* for short, came out to see what the dogs were sensing. Thembi had just returned from the city to find out how the children were doing. She could not believe Zee was alive when she heard his voice. In disbelief, she ran back to the kitchen to find a flashlight. In a few moments, she returned, and Zee advised her to turn off the flashlight. In tears, Thembi fell into Zee's arms. Knowing that soldiers could be around, Zee asked to go to a detached room where he could hide. She opened the room and locked him in there while she warmed water for a bath.

Detached Room

She put water in the bathtub, provided a pair of scissors and a shaving machine, and cleaned clothes. Zee took his time to cut his hair and beard. His hair could have filled a ten-liter bucket, and Thembi disposed of the hair in the designated pit. He followed with a warm, refreshing bath and removed the old clothes that he had worn for three years. Feeling clean and refreshed, Zee returned to the detached room to hide again.

Shortly thereafter, Thembi returned with food. She served his favorite beef stew with green vegetables, beans, and cornmeal. Zee ate and cleaned up the plate. Thembi collected the dishes and locked him in for the night. Zee and Thembi would see each other and talk more the next day.

Early in the morning, dogs barked again as Thembi was about to start preparing breakfast. Lo and behold, there were soldiers. She greeted the soldiers and answered any questions they had. The male voices got Zee's attention, and he listened to the questions. In his limited Shona, he could hear that the soldiers were inquiring about dissidents. The soldiers moved around the yard and noticed that the detached room had a padlock on it. They asked why the room had a padlock. One soldier came close to the door, and Zee could hear the footsteps. Thembi told the soldiers that there was old furniture in the room and that there was no need to unlock it. She also told them about other rooms that had junk that she would check later in the week. After all, she lived in the city, and doors remained locked while she was gone. There was no reason to unlock the rooms daily. The soldiers were convinced and left without forcing the doors open. As they left, Thembi continued with her chores in the kitchen.

Zee's wife did not walk toward the detached room or come close to the detached room for fear the soldiers were watching. In the meantime, Zee was locked up in a hot, detached room the whole day. He went without breakfast until she opened the door to give him lunch. She called the dogs to follow her into the room with dishes in her hands as if she were going to feed them. She left the dogs in the room for a little while and called them out, locking the door behind her. Zee remained in the room, having his lunch.

Thembi returned to the room toward sundown to bring dinner. Zee apologized for the trouble he caused and explained that he wanted the wife to know that he was alive rather than hear the news from other people. Given that the soldiers were roaming around, Zee assured his wife that he would return to his hiding place. Thembi accepted the logic and advised him to leave before daybreak.

Zee did not tell his wife where he was hiding and where he would go, lest the soldier torture her, and she disclosed where he was. He prepared her to wait until normalcy returned. Thembi had to keep the secret for her own safety. He tasked her not to share the information with anyone else except his uncle in the nearest town. If she ever shared his whereabouts, she would risk her life, the uncle's life, and Zee's. After lengthy discussions deep into the night, Thembi got Zee a stronger pair of shoes, a newer shaving stick, and a warmer jacket, and Zee took a nap until dawn.

Return to the Cave

Thembi awoke Zee, and he got ready to leave. Zee assured his wife that he would see her again soon. Zee left, heading back to the cave. What a risk he had taken! In a way, it was good that the soldiers came as if to remind him to return to the cave. Being home was unsafe for him and his wife. If soldiers had not come, he would have relaxed and ended up in trouble.

Halfway through the journey to the cave, Zee saw soldiers drinking under a tree and speaking aloud. He hid, changed course, and sneaked away into the dark. He walked stealthily toward the cave but hid in the hills for a while. He did not go to the cave in case the soldiers followed him. He remained tucked in the hills until he heard the sound of the soldiers disappearing toward the road to the west.

At sundown, Zee made it to the cave. What a scary adventure it was to risk going home. He almost got his wife into trouble and risked arrest and likely death. He had made an unwise decision. The experience taught him to slow down and accept the cave as the safest place he could possibly be under the circumstances.

Protection

As he reflected on his carelessness, he realized that he had been warned not to leave the cave but ignored the advice. As if he had not learned anything after the close encounter with the soldiers at Joe's home, Zee recalled that when he tried to leave the cave, he heard voices. It was the sound of people talking as if they were coming to the cave, but he could not see anyone. He retreated into the cave several times to hide from anyone possibly coming toward it. When the sounds faded, his mind told him to leave the cave and head home. Regret subdued him until he fell asleep. Looking back, he realized that the people's voices were a way to keep him protected in the cave, but he ignored the sign and left the cave. What a stubborn man he was to risk his life again!

It dawned on him that if he acted right and hid until the situation improved, he would be safe in his hiding place. After all, the people who knew his situation could not snitch because they, too, could get into trouble. He had confidence in Joe and his wife, the only two people who had seen him after his escape. Ultimately, it was Joe, Bongi, Zee's wife, Thembi, and Zee's uncle who knew Zee's predicament until a semblance of normalcy returned.

Chapter 9
Return Home

While Zee sought refuge in a cave like an animal, fellow defenseless civilians were losing their lives in huge numbers. People were dying for the same accusation he was evading. The soldiers targeted adults and picked, pursued, and killed whomever they wanted and for whatever reason. There was no one to stop the bloodthirsty killers. The brains behind the killings wanted to annihilate anyone who allegedly supported dissidents in Ndebele-speaking regions. Published articles and newspapers reveal that thousands of lives were lost during the Fifth Brigade purge. Land degradation continues to expose human remains in shallow graves, with more bodies piled in disused mine shafts. Zee's body could have been buried in a shallow grave, thrown into a mine shaft, or worse, had it not been for his courage to flee the torture camp.

Those barbaric acts occurred out of tribal malice. Black Shona soldiers killed fellow Black civilians who spoke a different language. The calculation was to eliminate the Ndebele-speaking tribe in the southern and central regions to weaken ZAPU, the main opposition party that had fought the Guerilla War like the ruling party. The innocent civilians were a threat to one-party rule and a hindrance to total control by the ruling Shona elite. It was after butchering enough people and securing political influence that the ruling elite desired to engage in talks with the opposition to produce a truce granting amnesty to dissidents who had contributed to the purge in the first place.

The end of the dissident menace meant that the soldiers would stop killing people under the pretext of fighting the enemy of the state. As hoped, the ruling party and the opposition reached an agreement and offered amnesty to the dissidents. The amnesty also pardoned those hiding and detained for dissident-related accusations. The amnesty provisions applied to Zee, who allegedly supported dissidents whom he never met. The amnesty spared Zee for allegedly feeding dissidents and for fleeing from torture.

After scary close encounters with soldiers at Joe's home and his own home, Zee exercised caution and avoided rushing out of the cave lest soldiers trap and kill him before their departure to the barracks. There was nothing to stop the soldiers from doing whatever they chose to do on their way back to base. After all, the killers had become used to butchering defenseless souls, and they would continue with their killing habits if they so chose.

The question was whether there were dissidents in the first place. Who were those people, what was their goal, how big was the group, who was their leader, who provided the dissidents with arms, and who was sponsoring them? If dissidents existed, why were there no reports of dissidents being apprehended and tortured in public to deter the collaborators? For a right-thinking man like Zee, something sinister was going on, and the best he could do was to keep hiding until he heard something new from Joe.

Dissident Menace Ends

The authorities designated points where the dissidents would assemble. The former thugs would present themselves with their weapons and be accepted without question. They were exonerated of all wrongdoing. The people they killed and how they killed defenseless souls, the homes they burned, the women they raped, and the trouble they caused were dismissed as if nothing ever happened in the first place.

There was no assembly point established near Zee's hiding place or his home. He would have to travel to see the people who brought him so much suffering and invited death to the region. He genuinely wanted to see what dissidents looked like and hear what they would say about what they did. The nearest assembly point was far from Zee's home, and it would have been a waste of money to travel to the nearest assembly point to see people who had already squandered his time and life.

A myriad of questions bombarded Zee's mind without answers. If it could be so easy for the government to welcome dissidents at the assembly points, what other arrangements did the government have with dissidents? Who were those people? Why did the government not stop the dissident menace earlier? All the same, Zee was on his way out of the cave to be free once again. After the amnesty, there would not be any more questions from the soldiers demanding self-incriminating answers to justify killing defenseless civilians at random.

At the same time, the soldiers returned to the barracks, and the Fifth Brigade disbanded. The ruling elite had accomplished its mission and cleansed the region of undesirable elements with "rain that washes away the chaff." Gukurahundi had lived up to its name and eliminated the opposition. At that point, Robert Mugabe and the ruling elite had achieved the overarching goal of establishing one-party rule in the country.

The top commanders received honors and promotions for butchering the helpless men, women, and children of Ndebele descent. It was shameful and a classic display of cowardice for soldiers to kill innocent people as they did. Zee wondered aloud how the soldiers could sleep at night after committing such atrocities and causing anguish in the region. How could such a bizarre situation make sense to the ruling elite?

As for dissidents, it remains unclear what happened to them after the amnesty. Questions about dissidents still linger without answers. What did they gain by roaming around the southern region and getting innocent people killed? Were the dissidents paid to aid the state in accomplishing its mission?

Even more shocking were reports that barely 200 dissidents operated in Matabeleland and parts of the Midlands. In the process of hunting down 200 dissidents, the Fifth Brigade killed over 20,000 Ndebele-speaking civilians. Where was the logic in such an operation? There was none; it was madness.

The dissident issue puzzles one when one draws insight from literature that reveals that a brigade consists of a few battalions. In other words, the Gukurahundi brigade trained between 3,000 and 5,000 soldiers to hunt 200 dissidents. During the course of the tragic exercise, the soldiers killed over 20,000 defenseless Ndebele civilians. The amount of force used on civilians far outweighed the dissident threat. Clearly, the Fifth Brigade had a far more sinister motive than to pursue a mere 200 thugs. The goal was genocide.

How could defenseless villagers resist dissident demands for food at gunpoint? If they cooked, they were killed. If they refused to cook, they still got into trouble. Furthermore, how could the villagers know that the soldiers were trailing the dissidents? The soldiers would confront those who collaborated with the dissidents. Like a joke, the soldiers would provide specific names of individuals forced to cook for the dissidents, what they cooked, the time of the meal, and the number of dissidents fed. Where did the soldiers get that information, and what did the soldiers expect the villagers to do? Once the villagers fell into the trap, the soldiers would descend on the villages under the pretext of pursuing dissidents and inflict unimaginable cruelty.

There were instances where the accused villagers dug their own graves, and other members of the community buried them alive. Upon covering the mass graves with dirt, other villagers jumped up and down on the graves. After burying fellow villagers alive, those who danced on the graves were shot and buried in shallow graves. In addition, soldiers cut up pregnant women to see what the babies looked like in the wombs. The soldiers forced the same women to pound babies with a pestle and mortar. Still, others had hands tied to their backs and were thrown into disused mine shafts, alive. There were no reports of such cruelty to dissidents, but why not?

Zee did not hear of a dissident ever being apprehended, paraded, or humiliated in the villages. How could they evade soldiers during the purge against the Ndebele-speaking tribe? Were the dissidents that creative to evade the soldiers throughout the purge? Ultimately, Zee's opinion was that the Gukurahundi campaign was an unwise undertaking executed by a useless brigade that could only kill unarmed civilians. Why would a trained military outfit fail to defeat 200 thugs and turn against unarmed men, women, and children instead? What kind of government kills defenseless citizens?

Zee's mind flashed back to his torture at Silobi. He remembered men gathered at the torture camp like sheep ready for slaughter. He pictured himself being led to torture, and at that point, his mind could not accept that kind of abuse. He was sad for those who remained in the camp, hoping for forgiveness from soldiers who knew no mercy. He had never allowed anyone to bully him, and he would not allow the Fifth Brigade soldiers to violate him either. Though helpless at gunpoint, Zee would not have allowed the soldiers, who were small enough to be his children, to expose his private parts and attach their toys to his naked body. He made up his mind that if he were to die at the camp, he would have killed one or more of the soldiers as well. Before he could fight back, he fell unconscious. After regaining consciousness, he fled to the cave.

Farewell to the Cave

One December evening in the fourth year of Zee's hiding, Joe brought food. During the meal, he broke the news that the government had granted amnesty to dissidents and all those accused of collaborating with dissidents. Joe assured Zee that he was free to leave the cave and return home. Zee was skeptical of the report and reluctant to leave the cave that had provided safety during the difficult time. He chose not to leave immediately but monitored the situation for another week.

Joe still kept bringing meals in the evenings. He would reassure Zee that it was true that the government had pardoned the dissidents. The armed men were assembling at designated points around the region. That meant Zee could leave the cave and return home. Two weeks after Joe broke the news about the amnesty, Zee collected his belongings, bid farewell to the cave, and went to sleep at Joe's home.

The next morning, after breakfast, Zee thanked Joe and Bongi for their hospitality and their commitment to his welfare and bid farewell. Joe volunteered to carry Zee's belongings in a plastic bag and accompanied him toward his home. After about a mile, Joe handed over the belongings to Zee. They shook hands, and Zee thanked Joe once again for all the sacrifices made, and they parted. It was an emotional separation after a strong bond was established over the period Zee hid in the cave.

Zee followed the main road toward his home, still fearful of meeting soldiers and others. He avoided contact with other people by getting off the road whenever he heard voices coming in his direction. At that point, he was unprepared to meet people and explain himself, but to go home and start life all over again. Stories of his abduction and escape would come later.

Coping with loss

His wife heard of the amnesty and pondered how to get Zee back home. Little did she know that Zee had also heard and was making plans to return home. He arrived late in the afternoon to a joyous welcome from his wife, Thembi. Simply, seeing his wife again was like a dream. It was comforting to be back, but a lot looked absurd and unrealistic.

The desolation was apparent around Zee's home, and his heart sank. Among other things, the main house had broken doors and windows. "Could there be anything left inside?" he wondered. To his surprise, his wife went into one of the rooms and returned with a chair. Shortly thereafter, she brought a glass of water. Sitting on the chair to relax outside felt strange. Drinking water in a glass was another surreal experience.

Looking further away from the house, the crop field lay covered with thorns and weeds. There were no animals in sight. The wire fence that Zee mounted before his arrest was gone, and the yard was bare. He could tell there was a loss and that all his sacrifices had come to naught. Perhaps, with a changed mindset and hard work, he could start again.

Zee and Thembi listened to the news and got answers to some of the questions that tormented him in the cave. The next sticking point was whether the pardon granted to dissidents and those imprisoned for feeding the dissidents made such people eligible to return to work. He needed the matter resolved quickly in order to receive income and start rebuilding his life. He chose to relax for another week before heading back to the school where he last worked before his abduction by the soldiers. No one saw him, and no news spread about his return.

According to plan, the following week, he visited the school to make inquiries about returning to work. The head of the school could have run out of the office in disbelief. He asked if Zee was real, for he and others had received reports of his death at the hands of the soldiers who abducted him. He became an instant celebrity as other teachers saw him and ran out of their classes to greet him. All who greeted him were fearful but happy to touch his hands as if to confirm that he was a real person.

The head finally had the courage to welcome him into the office and asked him about where he had lived for the last four years and how he had survived. Zee was uncomfortable with the questions about his ordeal and asked for more time to respond. Rather, Zee asked if he could return to work. The head welcomed the idea and advised him to report to the district education office. At the district office, he would confirm his return and request reinstatement. Zee was grateful for the advice and made plans to visit the district office.

The trip created an opportunity for Zee to meet his uncle, who worked at the district office. The uncle was one of the four people who knew about and kept Zee's ordeal a secret. Without wasting any more time, Zee traveled to the education office the next day. His arrival at the district office shocked his uncle and colleagues. Ultimately, the district education officer confirmed that Zee could return to work immediately. He filled out forms and left to be with his uncle for a formal reunion.

Zee was grateful that his uncle acted maturely and never told anyone about his situation. The uncle helped him get back on his feet and advised him to report himself to the police to allay questions and ensure his safety. The police, in turn, sent him to the governor, who confirmed that he was safe and had rights like any other citizen.

Zee had escaped slaughter at the torture camp. The young soldiers hiding behind the camouflage and guns could not end his life. His death would come some other way, not through abuse, torture, and lies. He realized that the overzealous soldiers forgot that they, too, would die just like the people they butchered. Even the leaders who planned the genocide along the chain of command would die too. Here he was, back home, to live like a human being, unlike an animal in the cave. At last, Zee was out of the cave to begin life anew.

Chapter 10
Rebuilding

Zee returned to an empty home. Most rooms were vandalized, and assets were stolen. Blankets and clothes were gone. Kitchen utensils disappeared. The beds were missing. Cows and goats had gone astray with no one to mind them. It was a loss expected from a deserted home. The most disturbing part of the story was that the soldiers and a "neighbor" conspired to force Zee to leave home. Nevertheless, the truth stands that Zee did not feed dissidents, and no amount of ruthlessness could coerce him to confess falsehoods. He had done no wrong but was taken away from his family, inconvenienced, and impoverished.

When the killing ended, the soldiers returned to the barracks and got bonuses for eliminating those who threatened the status quo. Families robbed of parents and heads of households like Zee had to start from scratch. There was no help whatsoever from the state. There was very little he could do to change the situation except rebuild his home. As for livestock, he would gather the few animals left and restock them. Begrudgingly, he sat down to map out a recovery strategy.

The first step for Zee was to return to work and forward a token of appreciation to Joe prior to rebuilding his homestead. Gathering his children from their hiding places would be the next step. Replenishing stock would follow. It was also critical to plow and produce food for the family. After settling down, Zee would later relocate. He liked the area where he lived before the trouble with soldiers, but he no longer felt safe following the betrayal.

While hiding, someone vandalized his homestead. Strangely, no neighbor identified the betrayer or those who vandalized property and stole animals. How could that be? The place had become unsafe, and he could not trust the neighbors anymore. He had seen what trust meant to Joe while hiding in the cave. No one in the community had risen to Joe's level of trust, and for that reason, he planned to move away from the current neighborhood. Memories of Joe prompted him to look for ways to express gratitude to a man who stood by him through the most difficult phase of his life.

Appreciation to Joe

Joe was always present and available to talk to Zee. Each time Zee met Joe, they discussed many issues, leaving Zee informed about current issues. In addition, Joe performed rituals to keep Zee safe from soldiers who were out to kill him. Joe willingly shared food to keep Zee alive. Joe never complained about the cost of food but brought something to eat every night. He shared blankets. He shared his time and walked with Zee to the shrine and back to the cave at the height of Gukurahundi and dissident activity. Zee and Joe hid together when soldiers patrolled close to Joe's home. In short, Joe cared for Zee.

The struggle to keep Zee safe established a strong bond between Zee and Joe. His friend Joe was prepared to do the unthinkable to keep Zee safe from the soldiers, who hunted him like an animal. There was no reason for Zee to die for a crime he did not commit. Therefore, Joe ensured that Zee had the basics needed to survive in the cave.

Zee's life in the cave was secure and remained a closely guarded secret until the end of the upheaval. Because of Joe's presence, sacrifice, and care, Zee survived the ordeal. It was for such selflessness that Zee decided to present Joe with a heifer as a token of appreciation. If Zee had found one female cow left, he would have presented that only cow to Joe for his sacrifice and good heart. As long as he retained employment, he would buy cows, and the herd would increase gradually.

Return to work

Zee returned to work in January 1988, where he taught 4th grade. His mind settled down, and he kept busy with his duties. He loved his job and enjoyed walking to school and back home without fear. He appreciated learning from students and guiding young minds into adulthood. Back in his job, Zee connected with people around him daily.

During breaks and on the way back home at the end of each day, Zee had company. Colleagues asked questions about Zee's ordeal. The response was always the same. It was a tough experience, and he was not ready to discuss it. He did not even ask other colleagues about their experiences with soldiers and dissidents while he was gone. Zee did not want to hear horrific narratives about the soldiers or dissidents. He did not want to know that soldiers returned to the school to look for him after he disappeared from the torture camp. He had no interest in armed men who caused unnecessary problems for him and other innocent villagers. The disturbances did not make sense, and he was not prepared to talk about evil. It was best to be quiet and process the pain silently. All who spoke to him knew Zee needed space to recover from the trauma. Colleagues eventually switched to other less stressful topics to make Zee feel accepted again.

After a month of returning to work, people stopped inquiring about Zee's experience. They soon realized that there was little information to draw from him. After all, Zee did not trust any of the colleagues and neighbors in the community, given that someone among them had betrayed him to the soldiers. That person wanted him to die from the soldiers' brutality. To Zee's surprise, colleagues started sharing their experiences while he was away.

There were disturbing stories that people shared that reminded Zee of the horror he experienced at the torture camp. It did not come as a shock that soldiers loaded people into houses, locked the houses, and set the houses on fire, letting everyone scream and burn to ashes. As people were burning to death, the soldiers stood outside the houses with guns, ready to shoot anyone who tried to break free.

Boys axed their parents to death. The soldiers inflicted unimaginable brutality on the boys, who axed their parents to death. The soldiers committed barbaric acts that no normal person could fathom. How could boys who axed their parents and cut them to pieces remain normal after the act? How could an individual remain sane and sleep at night after committing such savagery? To this day, many villagers who were forced to kill fellow men in barbaric ways are mentally disturbed and live as homeless outcasts.

Girls and women faced inhumane treatment as well. It was not surprising to hear of rape; the soldiers stripped females naked and sexually assaulted them in public. There were no words to describe the soldiers' brutality. The soldiers followed orders and acted in wicked ways. The training produced soldiers who brutalized the defenseless rather than defend the unarmed civilians. According to the soldiers, the civilians deserved the worst torture and the most painful death for supporting the opposition and feeding dissidents.

Dissident Atrocities

At the same time, the dissidents committed their share of atrocities. They killed people for reporting them to the soldiers. They killed people for working for the government. They killed people for going to towns and cities to buy food. They killed villagers who were reluctant to share the little they had, including clothes and bedding. Teachers were the chief targets for the dissidents.

The dissidents raped female teachers in front of students. They forced male teachers to march around the school naked in front of students. As if shaming the defenseless was insufficient, the dissidents beat some teachers to death.

Although the teachers outnumbered the dissidents at every school they invaded, they endured the abuse without resistance. To Zee, the teachers should have disarmed the dissidents and killed them. However, the brave individuals who tried to wrestle weapons from the dissidents, died alone without help from their timid colleagues.

If the villagers had been better organized, they would have teamed up to attack the dissidents and resist the abuse. Just like people at the torture camps, there was overwhelming fear that anyone who tried to resist torture would die alone. The majority of the detainees waited for mercy from soldiers who knew no compassion. The detainees knew that no such mercy would ever come but hoped for impossible miracles.

Zee was glad that none of the dissidents ever came close to him. He would have injured or killed the nearest dissident with any object in the vicinity. He would have attacked, killed, and buried the dissident who came alone to his home. After his hardships, no dissident or drunken soldier would terrorize him. He knew better and was more courageous to die in battle against misguided dissidents who dared harass him in his home.

The Homestead

Thembi, Zee's wife, had hidden family savings in a hole at the back of the yard. When Zee returned, she retrieved the money, and they had enough to start rebuilding. The family used the money to hire a builder to fix and remodel the existing structures. The builder charged them a modest amount, and they had little more left to purchase building and roofing materials. Zee and Thembi collected pit and river sand for reconstruction. When all materials were in place, construction began in earnest.

The plan was to revamp the home to create room to hide in case upheavals arose again. Thus, they added a room with a door leading out to the bush in the backyard. They added two other stand-alone houses to provide additional hiding. They improved landscaping and planted trees around houses, unlike in the past when the yard was bare, and soldiers moved around as they pleased. Zee remembered that they should not invest heavily in an area where someone in the neighborhood betrayed him and where their livestock disappeared without a trace. Rather, they would repair broken doors and windows on existing structures and then relocate. Within two months, the home returned to its original beauty.

Gathering Children

After the abduction, Zee's children fled their home to safety in the city. The girls were grown, and soldiers could have raped them and done the unimaginable. The boys were in upper primary and high school, and the soldiers could have misconstrued them as dissidents. At the same time, the dissidents could have attacked the boys for being government agents and inflict unimaginable savagery. The soldiers and dissidents alike would have shown horrific cruelty, especially after Zee's escape from the torture camp. After Zee's abduction, the children successfully traveled to the city and never returned home. It was safer to seek refuge in the city than risk torture, rape, and shame in the countryside.

Zee's wife remained alone at home in the countryside with no help or support. Occasionally, she checked on children in the city. The soldiers and dissidents could have come and beaten, raped, or killed her without anyone knowing. Thembi was determined to keep her home and die if need be. She was prepared to face the dissidents and anyone inquiring about dissidents. Periodically, the soldiers came to harass her, but they did not harm her. No dissident ever came to demand anything from her.

Whenever the soldiers came, they accused her of supplying dissidents with drugs, and she would always tell the soldiers to go back to their sources of information. The information was maliciously designed to trick her into fleeing so thugs would come to plunder the homestead. The soldiers had used a similar strategy to abduct Zee, but that approach would not work to force her to abandon her home. Each time soldiers pounced on Thembi's home, they demanded marijuana as if she were involved in drug trafficking. She scoffed at the demands and unequivocally denied involvement in any form of drug trafficking. The soldiers would leave infuriated by the lack of evidence of drug trafficking and the absence of information about Zee's escape from the torture site.

Regardless, the children grew up in the city. The two older girls completed teacher training and helped their younger siblings. By the time Zee returned, the three younger children had completed high school and ventured into different trades. It was gratifying to find all children grown with careers. The children would help Zee settle down and contribute whatever they could to rebuild their home. With help from the children, he would use his earnings to restock.

Restocking

Left alone without a husband and children, Thembi had to fend for herself. She needed to fetch water and cook. She had to plow to produce food. The home needed cleaning. There were animals to care for. It was impossible to complete all the tasks alone. Survival under the circumstances demanded a different mindset.

The greatest challenge was caring for cows, goats, and donkeys. She did not know where they pastured, and she could not go out there and risk meeting soldiers and dissidents. The best she could do was care for animals that returned home in the evenings. She counted the animals that strayed as losses.

She stayed home and avoided going out as much as possible. Death was around her, whether she stayed home or moved out to fetch firewood or water. The concern was that the soldiers or dissidents would invade her home at any time. The other concern was that the criminals in the neighborhood would pounce on her whenever they wanted since they knew that she lived alone. The same thugs would break into houses and drive animals away whether she was home or away. Thembi found herself in a helpless situation.

Occasionally, Thembi would visit the children in the city. Each time she returned from the city, something would be out of place. Certain items would be missing or misplaced. There was little Thembi could do, and there was no one to ask. Asking would be a way to start gossip in the community and invite trouble to the homestead. Keeping quiet in pain was the safest step to take.

It looked unreal that the authorities could permit such cruelty to develop without regulation. "Were the authorities aware of what was going on and that the soldiers were doing as they pleased?" Thembi would remark about the people behind the military purge in the region. Little by little, cows, goats, and donkeys disappeared, with nothing she could do to bring the animals back. Only a small number of cows and goats remained. Over 30 cows went astray without a trace. Out of 20 goats, only five remained. Out of eight donkeys, only two remained. Only chickens multiplied under Thembi's careful watch at home. It was heartbreaking to see the desolation that Zee met when he returned. Despite the apparent loss, there was no time to mourn but to rebuild.

After six months of employment, Zee started buying young female cows. In three instances, he purchased female cows with calves. By the end of the year, Zee had bought five female cows. The number doubled the following year when the heifers started producing young ones. Zee hired a helper to herd, vaccinate, and brand the animals. Further, he bought five female goats and added two female donkeys to prepare for the plowing season.

By the end of the first year of Zee's return, five cows had given birth to five calves. The herd has grown steadily since then. After twenty years, Zee has a huge herd of cattle. Goats have multiplied in number, and today, Zee boasts of over twenty goats. Donkeys have also grown in number to make plowing easier.

Producing Food

Left alone after Zee's abduction, Thembi could not manage the field. Rather, she started a small garden. The garden flourished with green vegetables, tomatoes, onions, and hot peppers. Soldiers would harass her for the garden. They accused her of feeding dissidents and producing marijuana, but she denied all the allegations. Without proof, the soldiers would threaten to return with a vengeance. Eventually, Thembi developed a thick skin, and no one could harass her. She talked sense into the soldiers, and they would depart hurriedly to avoid hearing more truth.

Zee returned home during the rainy season, but they could not plow with only two donkeys left. All of his plowing implements had disappeared except for two hoes. That meant buying new implements and raising donkeys to plow during the following season. That year, Zee and Thembi maintained the garden and used the two remaining hoes to till about one acre of land.

They dug holes and covered the seeds with dirt. While working, they shared endless stories. Once again, the couple reconnected while doing the manual work. They planted a variety of crops, including corn, pumpkins, beans, peanuts, and watermelons. Adequate rain fell, and the crop thrived, giving an abundant harvest.

The couple harvested several bags of corn, beans, and peanuts. They had enough watermelons and pumpkins to eat, so they sent the remainder to Joe's family and relatives in the city. The rest of the watermelons and pumpkins became food for the animals. Farming improved in the following year as donkeys increased. Work became lighter when the children returned home to help in the field. After three abundant harvests, the family met to consider relocating. The family gathering overwhelmingly approved of the idea of relocating to move away from the traitor in the neighborhood.

Chapter 11
Relocation

Considering the complications that arose after Zee's abduction, the family felt unsafe at their old home in Kalaza. The family could not trust people in the neighborhood, and there had to be a way out of the tension. The family had to flee from a traitor who gave false information to the soldiers, alleging that Zee had entertained the dissidents. Such an offense was so unforgivable that Zee was taken away to be killed. Miraculously, Zee managed to escape.

Inquiring about who betrayed Zee was unnecessary. The hope was that one day the family would know the truth. Determined to shame his enemy, Zee approached the local chief and asked for land twelve kilometers southwest of the existing home. The chief granted the requested land, and Zee resettled at Pani.

While preparing land for resettlement, the family would remain at the old home until the completion of the new home. The builder who renovated the home when Zee returned from hiding went to start work at the new location. The first structure was a three-bedroomed house with a room for parents, one for boys, and a third bedroom for the girls. The kitchen stood alone, a few meters away from the main house. Other structures would follow as needed.

Zee hired two men to clear and fence four acres of land for crops. It took several months for the two men to dig out trees, clear the field, and fence it. The next task was to cut wood and construct cattle and calf kraals. A distance away, they built separate enclosures for goats and donkeys, with room for extension as the herd of animals increased. While construction was going on, Zee arranged for a transfer to the local school where he was relocating.

In the third year after Zee's return from hiding, the family moved to a new location. Zee transferred and started work at the school in the new location. The workers demolished the old structures and moved the bricks and roofing material to the new location. Zee hired a big truck that made two round trips to ferry the bricks, roofing material, and furniture to the new location.

The helper and two assistants drove the animals to the new location. The move was slow because there were many young animals. The exodus started early morning to late afternoon. There were several breaks along the way, especially for the animals to drink water. At the same time, the assistants had refreshments.

When the animals arrived, Zee and his family were waiting to see the animals separate into their respective kraals. Relief fell on Zee, and he thanked the deity that had protected him in the cave. The same power had done so much good to him that he had resettled away from untrustworthy neighbors. "Surely His favor is on me," he remarked to his wife. There was hope for a better life in an area where he was unknown.

To be safe in the new area, he asked for a brief meeting where he would introduce himself to the community. A local leader arranged the meeting, and as planned, Zee introduced himself to the community. There was no one Zee knew in the community, and no one in the community knew Zee. That was a new beginning in a new location.

Zee settled into his new home. He found new pastures for the animals and quickly adjusted to the community. He would attend village meetings and exchange views with other men without divulging much about himself. He learned about problems in the community. He came to know individuals he could talk to and individuals he could not trust in the neighborhood. That was crucial information he needed to avoid the replication of problems from the previous community. In due course, some people in the community came to know about Zee's ordeal. One or two neighbors asked Zee about the rumor, and he dismissed the hearsay. He never discussed his past problems with anyone in the new community.

Work at the New Location

Zee also settled down as a teacher at Pani. The school was within walking distance of his homestead. It was healthy to walk after many years of sitting in the cave. Teachers and students were his neighbors, and he quickly adjusted to the school culture. The colleagues were pleasant and supportive. Rumors spread about Zee's troubles during the military purge and his subsequent escape, but no one had the courage to ask Zee about the experience. He kept his ordeal to himself.

The school day started early in the morning and ended early in the afternoon. This gave Zee time to grade assignments and plan for the next day. He would also use the afternoon to help with sports. Zee particularly liked soccer and joined the coaching department. The school had competitive matches with other schools in the district. Such activities helped Zee connect with other people: colleagues, parents, and children. Such interaction was therapeutic to ease Zee's traumatic experience during capture, torture, and escape to the cave.

The other comfort and recreation came from animals: cows, goats, and donkeys. Seeing his animals multiply was comforting to Zee. Caring for the animals, especially the young ones, calmed his mind. Interaction with the animals and their positive response brought him joy.

The proximity of the school made life even simpler. On his way back from work, Zee would come across some of his stray animals and drive them home. It took a while for the cows and goats to find their way home. During the first few months of relocation, Zee and his helpers went around the neighborhood looking for animals that had lost their way. Zee's young animals lost their way home, particularly when they blended with the neighbors' animals. It was a daily evening routine for Zee and his helpers to go around the neighborhood, fetching stray kids and calves. The practice continued until the goats, cows, and donkeys adjusted to the new home.

The blessings that Zee received upon his return from hiding never blinded him to Joe's kindness. He never forgot his friend. He did not cut ties with Joe after giving him a heifer as a token of gratitude for his sacrifices. During school breaks, Zee visited Joe to express gratitude for his sacrifice. After retirement, when Joe's health deteriorated, Zee was there to help his friend. Zee's visits continued every year until Joe passed away in 2017. After Joe's death, Zee visited Joe's family whenever he could. When Zee's health started failing, he sent occasional greetings to Joe's family.

Retirement

After teaching at both Kalaza and Pani schools, Zee retired in 2003. During his employment, he paid taxes and contributed toward his pension. The law of the land required every employee to contribute toward a pension. Zee was uncertain about the government's part in matching what the employee contributed. The monthly pension contributions were set aside for use after retirement until the death of the contributor.

Nine months before retirement, Zee filed for pension remittance. The process took time, and he received a reply after three months. To his disappointment, the letter asked Zee to fill out more forms and explain why there was a break in his employment. He was honest and indicated that he was hiding during the Gukurahundi disturbances. After a month, he received another letter informing him that the Pension Fund Department had declined his application on the grounds that he broke service in 1983. In essence, he had quit, and he should have applied for a pension when he stopped working. If he served a prison sentence between his abduction and when he resumed employment, the pension fund needed proof of incarceration. The pension department declared that it could not pay a criminal who hid from law enforcement in a cave during the military purge. If unsatisfied with the decision, Zee was free to travel to the capital city to explain his case in person. Going to the pension headquarters meant that Zee would be prepared to deal with an investigative unit to prove his innocence.

The application for a pension was triggering pain and anger for a crime he did not commit. Zee resolved not to entertain further persecution and stopped pursuing the matter. The developments meant that Zee had contributed in vain and could not receive his pension. His supposed crime was feeding dissidents whom he had not seen and escaping from torture for a crime he did not commit. If he had endured the humiliation and died, the pension department, an arm of the government, would not be dealing with the case of a dead man. Technically, Zee had lost his contribution as he had lost his assets during hiding. The question was why he would suffer so much under the hand of a Black government when Black people received their pensions under a supposedly oppressive White regime. Intense anger, resentment, and hatred toward the ruling elite built up within Zee.

Bitterness

The Pension Fund has withheld Zee's contribution to date. "Who would not be bitter at such nonsense?" Zee vented out loud! "Why would he accept such abuse?" "Where was the amnesty that the governor and other government officials offered to dissidents who committed atrocities?" Zee whined further. After what has happened since the amnesty, it is clear that the state wanted to pardon the dissidents who helped soldiers kill as many unarmed civilians as possible. The amnesty was a hollow gimmick designed to reward those who masqueraded as dissidents.

The deception made Zee very bitter. He was bitter at the accusation of feeding dissidents. He was angry with the soldiers for confiscating the bag of cornmeal he had for his children. He was bitter that he left his family without food. He was bitter about being tortured for a crime he did not commit. He remains bitter that the state forfeited his retirement contributions. He is furious that the state could not compensate him for the loss of property. He remains bitter that the state still refuses to pay for back injuries and kidney and urinary complications, including hearing difficulties sustained from torture. What the state did to him and continues to do is grossly unfair.

Despite the anger, Zee is grateful to be of a sound mind. The soldiers might have disabled his body, but his faculties are intact. He thinks clearly and knows right from wrong. The torture and the cave could not break him mentally. He is in control of his emotions and thinks clearly about his life.

Zee has a new home. His animals keep multiplying, and he has an income after retirement. He might have lost his retirement benefits, but he is surviving. The state, through the pension department, might still be withholding Zee's pension to punish him for escaping being bludgeoned to death at the torture camp, but he believes that those behind such evil will pay for what they did. Out of the experience, Zee has become wiser, more focused, and more hopeful to see justice done before he dies. He prays that he will forgive those who made him suffer and believes that he will move past the pain he endured.

Chapter 12
Looking Back

Zee retired to his home without a pension. The authorities had refused to release his retirement benefits despite the contributions Zee made during his active employment. He could not travel to the capital city to argue his case; he feared arrest for making inquiries, and for retelling the story about his escape from torture for a crime he did not commit. He made the decision to accept the denial and to survive without a pension. He would make a living from managing his stock and crop production.

Looking back at what transpired during the ordeal, what does it all mean to a defenseless teacher who was captured to be killed for a crime he did not commit? What does it mean for a man who lived like an animal in a cave for years? What does the survivor think about the hardship he endured long after his abduction and return from hiding?

First and foremost, no human being in the modern world should live in a cave. Seclusion, lack of human contact, absence of comfort, deprivation, and the perpetual fear of being devoured by wild animals can cause anxiety and destroy the human mind. Zee was not completely immune to those factors, and they turned him into a bitter man.

Who would not be bitter after such horrible treatment by an oppressor? Who would not be bitter about being accused of and arrested for a crime he did not commit? Who would not be bitter about being tortured to confess that he fed dissidents whom he never saw? Who would not attempt to flee and hide to save his life?

Despite the bitterness that built over four years in the cave, Zee had to return home to resume normal life. To his surprise, there was nothing normal about life outside of the cave.

The ruling Shona elite that wanted him killed was still in power. There was little sympathy to expect from such people for coming back alive. They might have allowed him to return to his former employer and contribute toward his pension, but they still found a way to deprive him of his retirement benefits.

The next question he pondered was whether the authorities would compensate him for the loss of property he incurred while hiding? If at all he committed a crime that warranted punishment, why did they not take him to court to allow him to prove his innocence? Why did the soldiers want to prosecute a case without evidence? Why would the soldiers be judges and sentence him to death without proving beyond a reasonable doubt that he committed a crime? Why would the soldiers attempt to torture him to death for a crime he did not commit?

During the amnesty, the state pardoned dissidents who killed innocent people. Why would the authorities pardon dissidents who killed people in barbaric ways and be vindictive toward an unarmed former school teacher? What was the purpose of the persecution after retirement? If someone with compassion, somewhere, heard Zee's cry for help, he would pursue the matter to the highest courts in the country and abroad to expose the ruling elite for violating his rights.

It was Zee's assumption that since the state pardoned the dissidents, the same state would compensate him for the loss incurred during the confusion. To his surprise, the amnesty only provided for his return to work but not for the disbursement of his pension or compensation for injuries stemming from being tortured.

Compensation for Injuries

Zee is currently at an advanced age. His health is failing. Residual effects from injuries sustained during torture are piling up. In addition to electrocution, the soldiers pulled Zee's legs to touch his head. That contributed to his back injury, which has resulted in a curved back. He stoops when walking with the aid of a cane. He has shrunken and become smaller than he really is. At a glance, you see an old man with a deformed back. He jokes, "They beat me to look like a comma!" Chiropractors recommend therapy, but Zee has no money for the service.

In the current economy, the little he has from selling cows is sufficient only for daily sustenance but inadequate to cover medical expenses. He cannot even afford painkillers and survives on traditional herbs. In addition to back complications, Zee has hearing difficulties.

Hearing Loss

The soldiers beat and kicked Zee all over his body, including his head. The blows were severe enough to affect the ears. The more the soldiers kicked him, the less he heard of what they were saying, leading to more savage beatings. Consequently, Zee lost some of his hearing.

He noticed the difference in hearing with the right ear while in the cave. At some point, the right ear was blocked off, and he could not hear anything, even in the silence of the cave. Hearing in the right ear gradually improved toward the end of his stay in the cave.

When he returned to the classroom, he could hear when students raised their voices and made noise. His hearing, however, got worse when he retired. The ears could no longer process low sounds. When he inquired about hearing therapy, the costs were prohibitive. He cannot afford a basic ear examination and ear cleaning. The condition is getting worse, and anyone speaking to Zee must raise their voice for Zee to hear. His hearing problem causes him to respond incorrectly to what others say. He gets embarrassed but excuses himself prior to speaking.

His voice trembles and his facial expression conveys anger when he recounts inconveniences that have befallen him as a result of unwarranted arrest and loss. Out of frustration, he retorts, "Why expect anything positive from such insensitive monsters?"

The state makes Zee's situation appear as if he is responsible for the problems he faces. The status quo suggests that it was Zee's fault that he lost his property for feeding dissidents. He has to suffer for embarrassing the state and for escaping from trained soldiers. The state would not compensate such a person. His contribution belongs to the state. In fact, he should have died rather than expect benefits from the state. Why would he expect compensation for the loss incurred during hiding? Why did he hide in the first place? Why did he not surrender himself to the soldiers and be bludgeoned to death like other members of his tribe? What compensation does he expect for pain and suffering? In Zee's mind, the state will always find excuses to deny him compensation and retirement benefits.

Litigation

If funds permitted, Zee would engage an attorney to argue his case in a court of law. A lawyer could convince the judge to order the state to compensate Zee for pain and suffering, loss of property, and retirement benefits. If, on the other hand, the state strongly feels that Zee has a case to answer for hiding from unwarranted torture, then the state should take the matter to court. It is in court that legal minds would review the case and determine the right course of action. The argument is that if the government could pardon dissidents, why punish Zee when he did not kill anyone? It does not make sense to pardon killers and punish a man for a crime he did not commit, especially when there is no proof that Zee committed the crime. If called to appear in court, Zee is ready to defend himself and prove his innocence.

Further, what good has the state done with his pension contribution when the economy is in shambles? There is massive unemployment. Poverty is rampant, and young people do not know what it means to earn a wage. Health delivery has collapsed. The roads are full of potholes. Power outages are daily occurrences. Poor water supplies cripple cities and towns. The massacre of the defenseless was of no benefit to the country. Nothing good came out of killing people and driving others to caves except to keep the ruling elite in power.

As Zee reflects on his experience years after his abduction, he sees the blind leading the blind. He sees the country going to the dogs. He sees failure. He sees misery around the country. He sees incompetent, ruthless leaders lose respect in the region and around the world. He prays that the leaders pay for their sins. He prays that he gets compensation for the pain he endured for a crime he did not commit. He prays that all the people killed for speaking a language different from the ruling elite get compensation and decent reburials. Zee has a message for his betrayers, his captors, the ruling elite, the remnant of the Ndebele tribe, and the international community.

Message for Betrayers

Zee never frequented local liquor stores. He did not visit neighbors' homes and was not curious to find out what was happening in the neighborhood. He had no time to discuss politics with his neighbors. He did not think anyone in the neighborhood would be interested in knowing who visited his home, who passed by, and how long the guest spent at his homestead. Much to his surprise, someone was monitoring Zee's movements, watching what he was doing, who visited his homestead, and when individuals visited. Instead of reporting what was happening, the betrayer imagined what was going on at Zee's home and decided to misrepresent the information to the soldiers. The distorted information was news that the soldiers wanted to hear. They did not care whether the information was true or false; they acted on the matter quickly without weighing the legal ramifications.

Despite the threats and verbal abuse, Zee kept wondering who could have betrayed him. Zee gathered the courage to ask the soldiers the name of the person who told them that he had fed dissidents. The answer was that they knew he fed the dissidents, but they could not reveal a name or explain how they knew.

After rounds of torture, Zee escaped without information about the person who betrayed him. If he had waited for soldiers to return from a break during the soccer game, he would have died without knowing the individual who betrayed him. Escaping without information was better than dying without information.

Zee still hopes that one day he will get a clue and face the individual who wanted him killed for a fictitious crime. As to the remedy for the betrayal, Zee wants a confession from the person who lied to the soldiers. He is ready to meet the individual and understand the motive for such betrayal. He believes the bitterness and anger in his heart will disappear if he sees the person confess. Zee is also ready to face his captors before he dies.

Message for Captors

Zee remembers his four captors. He believes that he could identify them if given a chance. He is not afraid or too angry to face the ex-soldiers whose brigade disbanded after the amnesty. He hopes to see the soldiers unarmed and ask them questions. He wants the soldiers to be brave enough to face him, talk about what they did, and apologize for what they did, if possible. He would like the soldiers to confess that they massacred people under orders. He also knows that the government would never apologize. To that end, each soldier must narrate his killing adventures in graphic detail. Knowing how the soldiers killed innocent people should bring closure for the loved ones.

Further, Zee would like his captors to explain the motive for harassing him the way they did. How could they treat him like a criminal when he had not committed a crime? If he committed a crime, why did they not take him to court and produce the evidence they had? What happened to the bag of cornmeal they confiscated? If they still feel he has a case to answer, why not take the matter to court? Do they know the kind of suffering they put him through to pretend that problems ended when the brigade disbanded? Zee wants to know what he did to deserve the torture and inconvenience he endured.

In retrospect, Zee also wants to tell the soldiers about the good that has come to him from the abduction. He wants the soldiers to know that he survived to tell his story to the world. The former soldiers must also know that even if they withhold information regarding who betrayed him and what they did during the massacre, they too will die or disappear like the very people they killed. As the Bible states, "Whoever sheds the blood of man, by man shall his blood be shed" (Genesis 9:6, Revised Standard Version). The soldiers must know that the ruling elite that sent them to kill thousands will one day hunt those same soldiers like animals and kill them as they did with defenseless civilians. Without fear, Zee wishes to see the soldiers pay for what they did.

He has lived long enough to see his country deteriorate after independence. He has seen the murderers fail to run a vibrant economy right before his eyes. He has seen education collapse and school buildings fall apart. He has seen the state that trained a brigade to kill unarmed men, women, and children fail to maintain roads and provide water to the citizenry.

He is no longer fearful. He has nothing to hide. He has nothing to lie about. The truth is that the ruling elite that was behind the mass killings has failed to run the country. Anyone looking can see what is going on. With the information he is giving the world, Zee knows that in his old age, the state agents could try to kill him as a way to silence him, but he is ready to tell the truth and die. If ruthless leaders like Adolf Hitler and Robert Mugabe could die, what makes the ruling elite and the soldiers who went about killing unarmed civilians think that they will live forever? They, too, will die like anyone else. All Zee wants is justice.

Message for the Ruling Elite

If the motive behind the military purge against the Ndebele-speaking people in Matabeleland and parts of the Midlands was to annihilate the entire tribe and allow the Shona tribe to blossom, then the ruling elite failed to achieve that goal. The same ruling elite butchered Shona-speaking people for voting for the opposition in the 2000s. To be clear, the Ndebele tribe was not the only enemy of the ruling elite. The enemy of the ruling elite is anyone who is ideologically opposed to the ruling elite, including Shona-speaking people. Under the prevailing economic climate, Shona-speaking people are suffering just like the Ndebele-speaking tribe. Simply put, the ruling elite wants power without opposition from both the Shona and Ndebele people.

The politicians create a rivalry between the two tribes to control the resources while everyone else, regardless of tribe, suffers. Once the masses realize that it is not one tribe over the other, it is only a matter of time before people rise up to oust the ruling elite. Before long, the two tribes will unite to fight a common enemy: the ruling elite.

Looking back, Zee feels robbed. He feels unjustly treated. It was unfair to abduct him for a crime he did not commit. It is unfair that his betrayer, whether dead or alive, remains a mystery. It is unfair that he never appeared before a judge to answer for a crime he allegedly committed. It is unfair that he has not received his pension. It is grossly unfair that he has not received compensation for the property he lost while hiding. It is unfair that he remains persecuted, yet the state pardoned the soldiers and dissidents who shed innocent blood. Why would the state apply amnesty selectively? Why persecute him for escaping barbaric torture and a painful death? What purpose did the amnesty serve if he remained destitute all his life for a crime he did not commit? Ideally, amnesty should offer justice to those who suffered loss and injury as Zee did, but things turned out differently.

He requests that the ruling elite pay for surgery to repair his spinal column and reposition the bones. His bladder, urinary tract, and kidneys also developed complications from torture, kicking, and gun beating. That is to say, Zee needs a thorough examination to rehabilitate the back, bladder, and kidneys. To that end, he wants the ruling elite to provide rehabilitation to the few Ndebele-speaking people who survived the military purge.

Message for the Ndebele Remnant

History shows that people repeat what happened in the past. It is strange that humans easily forget lessons from the past. They learn, forget what they learn, and repeat mistakes they ought to have learned. One would have thought that a man who sounded as intelligent as Robert Mugabe would have learned from

Nebudchanazeer, the King of Babylon, and Adolf Hitler, among other leaders from past generations. The one lesson from the past is that no matter how much an insane leader tries to eliminate a tribe or race, some people survive the purge. The few that survive would rebuild the tribe or race. Nebudchanazeer could not take all the children of Israel into captivity (Jeremiah 40:10-12, Revised Standard Version). Hitler could not kill all the Jews. Similarly, Robert Mugabe should have known that he could not kill all Ndebele-speaking people. Some Ndebele people would survive. Once again, history has proven a ruthless leader like Mugabe wrong. Zee survived Mugabe's wrath. He has rebuilt his home, and he has wisdom to share with the remnant of the Ndebele tribe.

"I cannot explain how I escaped and survived when some of my people could not," Zee remarks. Sniffing with tearful eyes, he looks out and urges the Ndebele to produce more children. He advises adults to tell children about what happened to those killed. He feels it is critical to tell children to resist oppression by other tribes. No matter how difficult the situation is, people must find means to defend themselves. It is unwise to expect pity from a rival who is out to kill members of a tribe. The tribe must stop the enemy from killing innocent civilians by all possible means.

Zee raises a mathematical analogy that the trained captives at torture camps should have used to neutralize the soldiers. He points out that a brigade consists of 3,000 to 5,000 men. Records at the end of the military purge indicated that over 20,000 people perished. That means the 5,000 soldiers split into tens of smaller groups and spread throughout the Ndebele region to face the population in the rural areas. These small groups of heavily armed men invaded villages, gathered, and killed large numbers of unarmed civilians. Imagine 10 soldiers gathering 100 people to kill, and 20 of the unarmed men and women were trained former fighters. How could 10 soldiers tie people's hands behind their backs and throw them into disused mine shafts one after another? Why would the trained ex-fighters not wrestle guns from the 10 soldiers and take them captive? There is no doubt that the soldiers would shoot some people in the tussle, but others would help to overpower the soldiers and seize guns, vehicles, and other equipment. That would have been one way to stop the madness.

The lesson here is that when soldiers raid a village and gather people to kill, they would rather shoot them from afar than come close and tie their hands behind their backs. If the soldiers come close, people must fight to disarm them, kill them, hide, and run away rather than allow the few soldiers to kill haphazardly. Zee was suggesting that if people had resisted wanton torture, the military purge could have ended earlier with fewer people killed.

Another lesson is that Ndebeles should respond to the situation as it arises. The political leaders that Ndebeles supported were in cities, while the people were dying in rural areas. The people should have revolted without orders from leaders hiding in cities. If they perished in the process of fighting to disarm soldiers, they perished. If they had overpowered the soldiers, they would have won and stopped unnecessary killings. The younger generation should never allow Black soldiers to kill fellow Black people. If the soldiers attempt genocide, they should know that the people will resist. People should not beg for mercy but use their numbers to overpower the misguided soldiers. Once the people outmaneuver the soldiers, the ruling elite should run or meet the wrath of the oppressed. "People must fight like our ancestors fought the British imperialists," Zee declared with confidence.

Zee concludes his advice by emphasizing that Ndebeles are militant yet loyal people, who descended from the Zulu warriors under King Shaka and Mzilikazi, the leader of the Matabele warriors. As such, they expect respect. If treated with respect, they reciprocate. If mistreated, the Ndebele people should not accept harassment.

If anyone breaks the law, let law enforcement play its part and arrest the criminals. Never should the state send soldiers to kill civilians like children's play. If the authorities ever send soldiers to harass civilians, the people should revolt and reject repression. Zee wants readers to know his experience and reject unjust arrests as he did. If it means hiding in a cave and living like a wild animal, so be it. If it means forfeiting a pension, so be it. If it means living to see the regime turn into a failure, let it be.

After all, the citizens have become poorer than they were under a White regime. It is not only the Ndebele tribe that is marginalized, but other groupings throughout the country. The majority Shona tribe struggles as much as the minority tribe does. Everyone else except the ruling elite lives from hand to mouth. The disgruntlement building up is like a volcano about to erupt. Zee appeals to the international community to intervene and avert bloody conflict between the ruling elite and the oppressed.

Conclusion

While Zee was languishing in the cave, Gukurahundi claimed over 20,000 Ndebele lives. Their remains rot in old mine shafts and shallow graves. The surviving relatives want to rebury their loved ones, but the state frustrates the effort. It is safer for the ruling elite to keep the dead where they are than to start exhuming bodies and pulling out skeletons from mine shafts.

It is known that some developed countries provided training for the new army after Zimbabwe's independence. Revisiting Gukurahundi would likely expose some of the countries that provided funding and training. The state can pretend that nothing happened, but survivors like Zee have information to help the international community intervene. He calls on the *United Nations* (UN) to put pressure on the ruling elite to acknowledge the genocide and rehabilitate the traumatized people.

Zee has information to help the UN understand the genocide and assist the voiceless. He is prepared to narrate his arrest for a crime he did not commit. He could paint a picture of how he escaped torture while others waited for an excruciating death. He is prepared to explain how he hid in a cave for four years while others could not escape. He is prepared to explain how he returned to work while other teachers like him never got a chance to return to work. He is prepared to articulate how he contributed toward his retirement while others never got a chance to contribute anything. Although he receives no pension, he manages to survive on a pittance while other civil servants, with their pensions as their sole source of income, continue to suffer beyond description. He wants the world to know that he is currently struggling with back injuries, urinary tract complications, and kidney problems with no help from the state that wanted to kill him for a crime he did not commit.

Zee has read about the role of the *International Criminal Court* (ICC), and he is convinced that he, too, could receive assistance. He does not fully understand how the body works, but he has a case that deserves world attention. If Slobodan Milosevic could be indicted for human rights violations, including the destruction of homes, murder, and rape during the Yugoslav wars of the 1990s, and Charles Taylor of Liberia still serves a prison term for similar human rights abuses, why would the ICC not try and charge Gukurahundi perpetrators for the gravest crimes against the defenseless civilians?

The ruling elite claimed that they did not kill that many people and shifted the blame to the soldiers, yet those same leaders planned the attacks and gave orders. Families that lost relatives have no power to open a case against the perpetrators of the genocide; however, the UN can gather evidence and forward the charges to the ICC for prosecution. People have information. People know where the soldiers buried their victims. People in the villages are willing to inform the world how the state butchered the defenseless civilians. Based on the information the villagers provide, the ICC should hear the arguments of state officials to fully understand the reasoning behind the genocide and provide an appropriate ruling.

Three decades after hiding in a cave for four years, the survivor still does not understand why the civilized and technologically advanced international community maintains silence about the Zimbabwe Genocide of the 1980s. The truth is that genocide occurred, and those responsible must face the wrath of the law. Zee is a living example of an innocent victim who escaped death at the hands of soldiers ordered to kill fellow Blacks. He was brave enough to flee torture and survive in the cave, like an animal.

He wants the world to know his story. He wants filmmakers to record his story and expose the evil that the powerful ruling elite hides. If he gets the means, he wishes to present his case to the ICC and have proceedings recorded for the world to see. From his submissions, the international tribunal would invite those implicated to defend themselves.

He seeks help to pressure the state to release his pension. He appeals to the international community to pile pressure on the state to fully compensate him for the loss of property incurred during the upheaval. The plea for help would not end without appealing for medical assistance to mitigate back injuries, bladder problems, kidney complications, and hearing loss inflicted during torture. Without apology, the survivor echoes the cries, screams, and shouts of thousands of innocent victims reverberating from disused mine shafts and shallow graves.

www.ingramcontent.com/pod-product-compliance
Lightning Source LLC
Chambersburg PA
CBHW040151160726
48006CB00014B/1698